FLIRTING WITH THE DEVIL

FLIRTING WITH THE DEVIL

BILL PRIDE

CROSSWAY BOOKS ☐ WESTCHESTER, ILLINOIS
A DIVISION OF GOOD NEWS PUBLISHERS

Bible verses are quoted from *Holy Bible: New International Version,* copyright © 1978 by the New York International Bible Society. Used by permission of Zondervan Bible Publishers.

Flirting With the Devil. Copyright ©1988 by Bill Pride. Published by Crossway Books, a division of Good News Publishers, Westchester, Illinois 60153.

All rights reserved. No part of this publication may be reproduced, stored in a retrieval system or transmitted in any form by any means, electronic, mechanical, photocopy, recording or otherwise, without the prior permission of the publisher, except as provided by USA copyright law.

Linotronic® Typesetting by TRC Enterprises, 10871 Sunset Hills Plaza, St. Louis, Missouri 63127.

Cover design: Karen Mulder and Tom Williams.

Cover photography: Bill Koechling.

First printing, 1988.

Printed in the United States of America.

Library of Congress Catalog Card Number 88-70694.

ISBN 0-89107-494-5.

TABLE OF Contents

Introduction   7

    Part One: In the Garden

1   Majoring on the Whiners   15
2   No-Fault Sin   23
3   In with the In-Crowd   33
4   If It Feels Good . . .   43
5   Hot Crossed Roles   55

    Part Two: In the Wilderness

6   Flirting with Pleasure   69
7   Flirting with Popularity   79
8   Flirting with Power   91

    Part Three: In the World

9   Walk Like a Man   101
10   The Big Picture   113
11   The Transformers   129
12   Scared to Life   145
13   Could Be Worse   159

Introduction

> *You adulterous people, don't you know that friendship with the world is hatred toward God? Anyone who chooses to be a friend of the world becomes an enemy of God. . . . Submit yourselves, then, to God. Resist the devil, and he will flee from you.*
> James 3:4, 7

Sue and Jim walked down the street arm in arm enjoying the warm, honeysuckle-scented evening air. They had been engaged for half a year and were very much in love.

As they ambled along, Nick came strolling towards them. Sue had heard about Nick. He was a playboy with a wild reputation who lived downtown. She never had anything to do with him. She was a lady, not a party animal!

Even so, as Nick walked by Sue sneaked a glance to see if he had noticed her. To her embarrassment she caught his eye. He smiled, satisfied that she was looking back. From then on, whenever they saw each other he greeted her. Eventually Sue began to smile and greet Nick back.

Jim left on a business trip, and time went on. Sue found she was "accidentally" running into Nick several times a day—and she became uncomfortably aware that sometimes she had arranged the "accident." Now Sue began to feel troubled. She knew Jim didn't want her to even *look* at Nick, much less encourage his attention.

"Jim would make a good husband," Sue thought. He owned a budding contracting business which already was making enough to support a family, and was building them a house. But Jim was not a particularly colorful companion. They went on walks, or out to eat at one of the neighborhood restaurants, or took in an occasional G movie. Although they had fun as a couple, no one would consider their times together glamorous.

On the other hand, Sue had heard that when Nick took out a girl, he really showed her a good time. He took her to the best restaurants, took her dancing, and sometimes afterwards took her to his apartment—though she herself wouldn't go there. He had bushels of money, dressed like a millionaire, knew all the right people, and was invited to all the chic cocktail parties.

One day Sue stopped and talked to Nick for a while. He was very charming and flattered her unmercifully. At the end of their conversation, Nick made it clear that if Sue gave him her telephone number she'd be hearing from him.

Somehow Sue didn't have the same joy in Jim she used to. Talking about the same old things, walking in the same old paths just didn't seem as pleasurable. She still loved him and didn't want to break off their engagement, but she didn't delight as much in his company as she had before she had noticed Nick.

What Has Happened to Our Joy?

The church is in the same condition with respect to her fiancé, Jesus Christ. The early Christians were madly in love with Jesus. They rejoiced at the opportunity to serve Jesus, and gloried that they were permitted to suffer persecution for His sake. They were so devoted to Jesus they turned the world upside down for Him.

The church has been blessed with other times like this. The Reformers were willing to die for Jesus' sake. Two centuries later, during the Great Awakening, the newborn Christians in England bore the looting and burning of their homes with joy. Evangelists like George Whitefield and John and

Charles Wesley exposed themselves to public abuse and ridicule. Some of their fellow evangelists were beaten, and one of them died after a rock thrown at him while he was preaching hit him in the head. But they continued preaching out of love to their Lord—and turned eighteenth-century England and America upside down.

As a whole our modern church doesn't have this kind of spirit. Several recent books say this is because the church has been seduced. And, in some cases, they are right. A number of churches have gone under to New Age thinking and psychology-as-religion. But most of what we could legitimately call "the church" is not into wild parties, decadence, or Satan worship.

Still, we are not turning the world upside down either. We are confused about doctrine and practice. Formerly solid doctrinal positions have become fluid. What used to be called "sin" now excites calls for compassion and total acceptance, or even for special privileges for those practicing it. We pick our way gingerly about, searching for a firm spot on which to stand. Meanwhile, polls tell us that the Christian kids who ought to be our pride and joy behave just as badly as their worldly peers. To put it charitably, the modern church is failing to be light and salt to our full extent—even in our own families.

Something is holding us back. Or, more properly, someone. Just as Sue had begun to allow Nick to interfere with her relationship to her fiancé Jim, the modern church is allowing Satan to throw cold water on our joy and delight in Jesus. We are not seduced . . . but we *are* flirting. We are not dead . . . but we *are* double-minded. Because we, like Sue, don't see below Old Nick's charming mask to his repulsive and rotten core, we have too often allowed him to distract us from our original mission. The result? Flat-footed Christianity without power to change lives or leaven society.

Between the Pier and the Deep Blue Sea

Flirting with the devil is like standing with one foot on the boat and one on the pier. The solid rock of the gospel is the immovable pier. The world is the boat. As long as the Western world was largely christianized, i.e. the boat was next to the pier, few people noticed their precarious position. Now that the boat has begun to move away from the pier, it is no wonder the straddlers are getting uneasy.

I am not the first to point out that the church has been flirting with the devil. A. W. Tozer and Francis Schaeffer, among others, warned us years ago. But ten or twenty years ago, only a few Christians with especially clear vision understood what preachers like Tozer and Schaeffer were saying. Today, now that we've come so far down Flirtation Trail, it's much easier to spot the fire and brimstone cooking up ahead. Satanic New Age religion has now come out into the open and is crusading for acceptance in all areas, including the church. The boat has drifted very far from the pier.

The Time Is Overripe (and So Is Satan's Rotten Fruit)

This all is depressing, isn't it? But we can actually have more hope now that the choices have become clearer. The fruit of past flirtation is coming ripe and some of us are starting to notice its unlovely smell. People are becoming aware of the devil's schemes and have begun writing books exposing them. Now, this book will explain how to fight back!

Satan is wily, but not original. He has just one basic strategy for tempting the sheep and one for the shepherds. Both have already been exposed in the Bible: once at the beginning of the Old Testament and once at the beginning of the New. We'll look at both through the temptation of Eve in the garden and Jesus in the wilderness. Then we'll look at God's strategy for combating the devil—a strategy that will work just as well now as it has for everyone who used it before us.

The Rest of the Parable of Sue (the Church), Jim (the Lord), and Nick (the Devil)

Oh, about Sue and Jim and Nick . . . One day, Jim returned unexpectedly from his business trip. Seeing Nick asking Sue for a date, he hid and listened, expecting to hear Sue telling Nick that she was engaged and unavailable. To his horror, instead she led Nick on, making it sound as though, although she couldn't go out with him this particular time, she would be delighted to sometime in the future.

That night Jim visited Sue and took her to task. "Don't you remember what happened to Sally and Ramona and Judy and all those other girls Nick has dated?" Jim reminded Sue. "You know how they ended up and how he disgraced them. And what about all the wonderful things we have been planning together? Our house is almost finished and we'll be able to move in soon. I love you, you know that, but Nick only wants to use you. He'll never cherish you the way I will. You can't have both me and Nick, so make up your mind."

Sue knew Jim was right. She knew what kind of person Nick was and that she had been foolish to flirt with him. Sobbing on Jim's shoulder, she told him she loved only him. "But I don't know *how* to get rid of Nick," she wept. "Every time I try to tell him about you, he comes out with some smooth line and confuses me. And I'm afraid of him, too. I know he has acted really nice to me lately, but I get the feeling that when I tell him it's good-bye he'll get angry at me. What should I do?"

Jim took Sue gently by the shoulders. "Don't worry, honey. I'll tell you what to say when Nick comes along with his smooth talk. And if you do what I tell you and he still bothers you, just let me know and I'll settle his hash."

Once we recognize how we have been flirting with the devil, and how it has weakened us, Christians today have a tremendous opportunity to take back ground that has been lost for more than a century.

Yes, Satan has his wiles, but Jesus has the answers.

PART ONE

In the Garden

Now the serpent was more crafty than any of the wild animals the Lord God had made. He said to the woman, "Did God really say, 'You must not eat from any tree in the garden'?" . . .

Genesis 3:1

1

Majoring on the Whiners

As a rule
  Man is a fool.
When it's hot,
  He wants it cool.
When it's cool,
  He wants it hot.
Always wanting what is not.

Author unknown

[The serpent] said to the woman, "Did God really say, 'You must not eat from any tree in the garden'?" The woman said to the serpent, "We may eat fruit from the trees in the garden, but God did say, 'You must not eat from the tree that is in the middle of the garden, and you must not touch it, or you will die.' "

Genesis 3:1-3

If you were cast adrift on a desert island, with no contact with the outside world except subscriptions to five or six Christian magazines, what picture of the world would you get? You would quickly learn that the world has a desperate shortage of choir robes, that you can tap HIDDEN TALENT as a writer of Christian children's books, that each and every Christian college is the very best place to attend, and that you too can earn $12,000 to $35,000 a year in an important ministry. If you get past the ads, you also learn that Christians today have unfulfilled needs. Lots of unfulfilled needs. Great gobs of enormous, gaping unfulfilled needs.

And this is odd, because although on your desert island *you* may have some serious unfulfilled needs (like food and water), the rest of us are sitting here in the richest nation on earth. We can *afford* choir robes and college educations! Further, money aside, we have no new social and emotional needs that Christians of centuries before didn't have. Yet we fill reams of paper and hours of counseling time complaining about issues that Christians didn't even know about a few decades ago. We have discovered burnout, mid-life crisis, and PMS. We are suffering from stress, poor self-image, and feeble relationship skills. Ninety-four percent of us are battling obesity or anorexia and almost all of us are fretting about our sex lives (that is, if you believe the magazine articles). Life on the desert island, by comparison, sounds pretty good.

Why these grunts and groans of discontent wafting through the fellowship hall? Why these endless articles and sermons about how to meet our ever-more-ersatz "needs" instead of the old-time emphasis on praising God and serving man? Why do we sound so dissatisfied?

Wait a minute! Who's that sneaking around the church, whispering sour nothings into our ears and striking sour notes in the choir? Could it be that we've been fooled again? Are we letting the devil, that old serpent, rob us of our joy? Have we fallen for the same pitch Satan gave Adam and Eve in the garden of Eden?

The First Labor Grievance

In the beginning management-labor relations were great. Adam and Eve had no complaints with their job. Working conditions were good, they were fond of their boss, the work wasn't too hard, their pay and fringe benefits more than cared for their needs, and each of them just adored his working companion. Sometimes labor has a legitimate grievance against management, but this was not one of those times.

Then Satan came along posing as the Great Advocate of the Underdog. "What's this I hear?" he inquired, simply reeking of compassion. "Is it true that your boss has you grubbing around in this garden for nothing?"

Now stop and think. If someone comes up to you and asked, "Why do you work for a boss who won't pay you what you are worth?" what is your first reaction? It doesn't matter if you're a corporate vice president earning $200,000 a year with perks; if you're a normal fallen human being, you will feel a momentary surge of resentment. You may stop later and say, "Wait a minute, I'm making a fortune and I like my job," but no one can help feeling that first resentment—and sometimes the feeling of resentment won't go away.

Adam, who according to verse 6 was standing right there next to Eve, didn't answer the devil. Eve, like a loyal employee, stood up for her Lord. "God doesn't pay us 'nothing,'" she responded. "We have more than enough trees to eat from. It is just the tree of knowledge of good and evil we can't eat from." But then she added just a hint of resentment, "and we can't even touch that one or we'll die."

Satan trapped Eve into saying, "God didn't hold back *all* the trees, just one." This translates to, "God isn't as unfair as you said, just a *little* unfair." By pointing out the one "imperfection" in the garden of Eden, Satan created a *false need*. Adam and Eve didn't really need the tree of the knowledge of good and evil, but from then on they felt like they did.

Satan does the same thing to us:

Satan: Why does God leave you in such wretched health?

Us: I'm in good health, really, except for this infected hangnail on my little toe which I admit has bothered me far longer than it should.

Satan: Why hasn't God recognized your contribution to the church?

Us: My Bible study has grown to fifty people and my adult Sunday school class is well attended, but in all this time they haven't made me an elder.

Satan: Why doesn't God let Christians have any friends?

Us: The church folk have been good to me, but since I went forward at that revival meeting, all my old friends are avoiding me.

Like any rabble-rouser, Satan gets formerly contented followers grumbling against the authorities—labor against management, citizens against the government, sheep against their shepherds, Christians against God. By pointing out the one small bruise on an otherwise sound apple Satan gets us to despise the whole fruit.

The Scarlet O'Hara Syndrome

Thanks to Satan's efforts, the Christian church today is definitely suffering from the Scarlett O'Hara syndrome. You remember Scarlett. She is the main character of Margaret Mitchell's *Gone with the Wind,* a book that was made into one of the most popular movies of all times. Though Scarlett had everything a southern belle could want and knew how to get just about anything she didn't have, she constantly craved more. Scarlett had beauty, youth, health, money, sex, power, children, servants, and Clark Gable (playing the role of Rhett Butler, Scarlett's husband), but she desired Ashley Wilkes, Melanie's husband, and could never rest content.

Because Scarlett could never be satisfied, she drove her husband to drink and finally lost his love. Too late she realized that her own husband Rhett was the man she really wanted. By chasing after fantasies she had lost what she had.

Doesn't this remind you of Adam and Eve losing paradise for the sake of a bite of fruit? And doesn't it remind you of the escalating tide of special interests and pressure groups within the church, each demanding its own agenda and none satisfied with the simple old gospel and the same old Lord?

These Men Are Full of New Whines

When the day of the congregational meeting had come, they were all in great discord in one place. Suddenly there was a sound like the rumble of an earthquake as all were filled with a complaining spirit and began shouting at once. The teenagers and their parents clamored for a youth pastor to organize their ski retreats. The mothers lobbied for a night out to get away from their families. Divorcées screamed for male companionship. A contractor bellowed that the parking lot needed to be redone.

The altercation soon spilled out onto the street and into an adjoining park which was sponsoring a concert. At the concert were worldlings from all walks of life who each one marvelled to hear the church folk speaking their language. "Here we are—married and divorced, young and old, male and female, yuppies and hippies—yet we each hear these people speaking in our own complaints the dissatisfaction of our hearts."

They were all amazed and were in doubt, saying to one another, "What's happening?" Others thoroughly disgusted with these church people said, "These men are full of new whines."

What's happening here? It's a bunch of squeaky wheels howling for some grease. The painful thing is they are all likely to get it. A full measure of attention, heaped up, shaken together, and running over, will the modern church mete out to those who whine for it.

God has a different way of dealing out His gifts and attentions. In God's economy, to those who have more is given, and those who have not lose even what they think they had (Matthew 13:12). Another way of putting this is that those who don't make the most of the little they already have are not eligible to be given more. "He who is faithful in little is faithful with much" is the Bible's way of looking at things. In other words, rewards go to those who *earn* them, not those who "need" them.

To the Victims Belong the Spoils

Losing Ground by Charles Murray is a book about the economic welfare system, but it applies equally well to a modern phenomenon—the spiritual welfare system. Murray contends that our current welfare system is not doing the job because of reverse incentives. Let's say that someone on welfare receives $400 each month from the government. He lives in government-subsidized housing, gets free medical care, and buys his groceries with food stamps. For all this he doesn't have to work at all.

After a while, someone who works nine to five or longer at minimum wage just to scrape by looks at these guys on welfare and sees that they are doing better than he is. So he gets himself fired and applies for welfare. Murray's argument is that an unforeseen side effect of our current welfare programs that were designed to help the poor is that they attract others onto it who were making it on their own before.

We do the same thing in the church when we coddle sinners.

Us: Bert, you have a problem with pornography, and a number of people in the church know about it.

Bert: Aw, shucks, you found me out. It's true. I just can't seem to get through a day without my copy of *Playboy*.

Us: You need counselling, you poor soul! Of course the elders won't discipline you. We won't even ask if you are sorry for your sin. As long as you submit to counselling we will consider that repentance enough.

All the people who know about this man's sin think he got away with it. Now Bert is getting special attention from the pastor. The pastor may not be helping this porn addict at all, but he is without doubt teaching the rest of the congregation that sin has no unpleasant consequences. Even if he preaches hellfire and brimstone from the pulpit, he has preached punishment-free sin by his actions.

We also tend to encourage spiritual dependency—the Permanent Counselee Syndrome. What better way to get the pastor's attention than to develop a big bad problem that takes hours of his personal time and attention? Or you can simply *threaten* to develop a problem—"Hey, we teens will stop attending if you don't entertain us with Pizza Pig-Outs and weekend parties"—and get fast, efficient service for your "needs."

In this way of thinking, nonbelievers—who have lots more "needs"—get priority over our fellow Christians, although God says we should do our good deeds *first* to our fellow Christians and then to those outside (Galatians 6:10, Romans 12:13). Obviously those without Christ need the gospel more than those of us who are already saved. But I have seen churches fall over backwards to serve the physical needs of potential converts, when church members with the same or greater real needs were ignored.

In one outstanding case, a neighborhood woman talked a church in which we were members into rebuilding her garage, painting her house, providing her a job, bringing her food, and spending hours holding her hand. This all-out effort took the resources of the entire church for about six months, and resulted only in the woman denouncing the church for not helping her more!

In the same church, we knew a young couple who had been struggling financially for years. They had several children, the wife had health problems, and the husband had a low-paying job. He spent every spare hour working to fix up their house, hoping to sell it for a profit that would enable them to get out of debt. The church showed an empty hand to this family, preferring to invest in an outsider who had never shown any disposition to faithful hard work. The Lord did provide through other means for this young family to sell their house and move to a better job. Shortly after they left the church, it dissolved.

Satan wants us to steal the resources of the spiritually productive to give to the spiritually unproductive. He wants us to indulge the whiners rather than to encourage them to make the most of what they do have. I am not saying we should never help anyone, but that we should help those who show signs of using our help wisely. Otherwise, we simply break the spirit of those who are struggling without encouragement to be faithful, as they see the unfaithful blessed while they are neglected.

Yes, God Is Kind to the Ungrateful and the Wicked, But . . .
God does not like whining. That is a fact. He considers ungratefulness and harping on what He supposedly hasn't provided to be a great insult to Him. Romans 1:21, describing how men become reprobates, states, "For although they knew God, they neither glorified him as God *nor gave thanks to him* . . ." The generation of Israelites that griped at God for forty years in the wilderness *died* in the wilderness. In contrast, Scripture tells us that "godliness *with contentment* is great gain" and that food and clothing are our only really basic needs (1 Timothy 6:6-8).

All this recent stress on the Christian's needs is playing right into Satan's trap. Whether we are encouraged to whine as a group (and the church is increasingly being divided into smaller and smaller special interest groups) or as individuals, whining is wrong. It destroys our joy in the Lord and leaves us open to further Satanic attacks.

Adam and Eve made a major mistake in letting Satan badmouth God without interrupting him. God is not a God who wants to frustrate our needs—He just happens to know that we have different needs than those Satan wants to tell us about.

Man does not live by bread alone, and Adam and Eve should have known that they did not live by fruit alone. But once they began to feel that God was unfair to hold back the forbidden fruit, they were prime targets for the next phase of Satan's attack. Once we start letting Satan tell us what our needs are, we're headed for trouble—as you will see in the next chapter.

♦ 2 ♦

No-Fault Sin

I know a funny little man,
  As quiet as a mouse,
Who does the mischief that is done
  In everybody's house.
There's no one ever sees his face,
  And yet we all agree
That every plate we break was cracked
  By Mr. Nobody.

Children's poem

"You will not surely die," the serpent said to the woman.

Genesis 3:4

It's take-it-easy time. After a hard day working, you're settled back in your easy chair reading what you think is a solid evangelical magazine. Then it happens. *Squish!* Suddenly you've hit a sinkhole. You're up to your ankles in The Typical Bad Evangelical Magazine Article!

For what to your wondering eyes does appear, but a paragraph like this:

> Beneath the facade of having it all together, many Christians are bundles of confusion, doubt, and fear. A religious veneer may hide a rotted core of lust, covetousness, pride, and self-deception. Scratch the surface, and you may find evidence of sexual abuse, family alcoholism, addiction to pornography, or bondage to various phobias and compulsions.

"To the Saints in Ephesus, the Failures in Christ Jesus"

Karl Marx couldn't have said it any better! Boy, if Christians are like that, then there is no point in being one, is there? You'd be better off as something respectable, like an international Communist terrorist or a member of the Mafia. (I didn't make up the magazine quote above, by the way. It was the lead paragraph of a book review in one of the most respected Christian family magazines.)

You know what I'm talking about. You've seen the Typical Bad Evangelical Magazine Article before. Here's how it goes:

- Virtually all, or at least a overwhelming percentage of Christians are engaged in

  ❏ adultery ❏ theft ❏ lying ❏ sexual abuse
  ❏ drugs ❏ wife-beating ❏ homosexuality
  ❏ grinding the face of the poor
  ❏ other _____ (fill in the blank).

- The reason this is not readily apparent to all of us, but only to those who write these articles, is that the typical Christian hides his festering sins behind the famous one-size-fits-all Evangelical Mask.

- Now that we know that all our born-again buddies are no-good bums, our duty becomes plain:

- *Totally accept the poor victims of sin as is,* encouraging them to retain their positions of authority in the church, while showering infinite contempt on anyone old-fashioned enough to believe Christians can and should be holy. For sin isn't really anyone's *fault*. None of us can have victory over any given sin, and none of us is responsible for giving in to sin.

"You Shall Not Surely Die"

Nothing ever is anyone's fault any more. We have no-fault auto insurance and no-fault divorce. Drunkards aren't to blame for their drunkenness. (The alcohol, like a measles germ, somehow floated into their bloodstream.) When a worker has an accident on the job, it's never his fault. In this self-esteem-ridden world, the cardinal sin is to imply that the disasters that happen to us could be the direct or indirect result of our own sinful or foolish behavior.

This whole no-fault attitude is an attempt to pretend God doesn't exist and it denies one of the basic facts of life: God punishes sin.

In Chapter One we saw Satan tempting Adam and Eve with the notion that God was being unfair to them. Once that seed was planted, Satan immediately began to water it. Even if God were unfair (which He never is!), Adam and Eve would have feared to disobey Him. So Satan unrolled this smooth lie—"You can disobey what God has said and you will not surely die."

Satan needs to blunt our fear of God's anger before he can successfully get us to turn against Him. As long as Adam and Eve feared death more than they desired the fruit, they wouldn't eat the fruit. So Satan invented the doctrine of no-fault sin. "Go ahead and sin. Nothing's going to happen to you. You have nothing to worry about."

What the devil said was a bald-faced lie, and Adam and Eve knew it. But once Satan had concentrated their attention on the forbidden tree and started them thinking that maybe God was unfair to forbid it, Adam and Eve were ready to theorize that God *might* have lied to them. They were all ears to hear what the devil would say next.

No-Fault News Is No News

Men have repeated the no-fault sin lie all through history. The Israelites said the same thing just before the destruction of Jerusalem. Jeremiah writes, "They have lied about the Lord; they said, 'He will do nothing! No harm will come to us; we will never see sword or famine. The prophets are but wind and the word is not in them; so let what they say be done to them.'" But God brought the Babylonians and destroyed Jerusalem.

The Apostle Peter writes about the same kind of people when he says,

> First of all, you must understand that in the last days scoffers will come, scoffing and following their own evil desires.

They will say, "Where is this 'coming' he promised? Ever since our fathers died, everything goes on as it has since the beginning of creation." But they deliberately forget that long ago by God's word the heavens existed and the earth was formed out of water and by water. By these waters also the world of that time was deluged and destroyed. By the same word the present heavens and earth are reserved for fire, being kept for the day of judgment and destruction of ungodly men.

"He's Making No Lists . . . Ain't Checking Them Twice, He Don't Even Care Who's Naughty or Nice"

Has the modern church bought the same lie? Well, how often do you hear sermons about God's judgment these days? Instead, sermons just overflow with sentimental ideas about God's love. God has been recast as Santa Claus—an updated Santa Claus who never leaves coal in a naughty boy's stocking. In this scheme of things, God exists just to bless us and help us and make us feel better. He totally accepts us the way we are, and merely wrings His hands mournfully when we go astray.

Noticing that the Bible teaches that this supposedly mushy God actually executes judgment on the wicked and casts unrepentant sinners in Hell, some have gone so far as to say, "The idea of an angry vengeful God is just a hangover from the less enlightened Jewish religion of the Old Testament. After all, the Jews believed that their God commanded them to completely destroy the Canaanites, even the babies. A 'loving' God would never do that, would He?"

Contrary to this theory, the Old Testament preaches the love of God right in the same verses that tell us God punishes sin. Just look at Exodus 34:6-7, for instance:

> And he passed in front of Moses, proclaiming, "The Lord, the Lord, the compassionate and gracious God, slow to anger, abounding in love and faithfulness, maintaining love to thousands, and forgiving wickedness, rebellion, and sin. Yet he does not leave the guilty unpunished; he punishes the children and their children for the sin of the fathers to the third and fourth generation.

And as for eternal punishment for sin being an *Old* Testament idea, most of what we know about Hell and the lake of fire came from the mouth of Jesus Christ, the loving Son of God, Himself. See Matthew 25:31-46, 8:11, 13:40-42, 47-50, 22:13-14, 24:50-51, 25:28-30, Luke 13:23-30, Matthew 5:22, 18:8-9, Mark 9:42-48, Luke 16:19-24, and John 15:5-6 for instance.

The Bible calls Jesus' sacrifice on the cross the highest expression of God's love. But if God does not punish sins, and can forgive them unilaterally out of love, then how did God show His love by throwing Jesus' life away as He did? Jesus' sacrifice was cruel and unnecessary if God could have forgiven us without punishing our sins.

Both Old and New Testaments teach that our God is loving *and* righteous. The God "who wants all men to be saved and to come to a knowledge of the truth" (1 Timothy 2:4) is also the God whose soul hates "the wicked and those who love violence" (Psalm 11:5).

The Sin-of-the-Month Club

Right and wrong, Heaven and Hell, and God's judgment have never been popular doctrines. Jeremiah got thrown into a muddy cistern for preaching them (Jeremiah 38). David got ridiculed (Psalm 69:6-12). "Fools mock at making amends for sin," says Proverbs 14:9.

Satan is at great pains to eradicate the teaching of responsibility for our own sins now as always, labeling it antiquated, naive, unloving, and dozens of other names. Instead, we are supposed to believe that salvation brings no power to change a sinner's heart attitudes or behavior. The poor victim simply can't help himself . . . and even God supposedly can't help those who can't help themselves.

Charles Finney, the famous evangelist, used to complain about people who talked about "poor sinners." In Finney's view, the compassionate friends of "poor sinners" were actually taking the heat off these sinners and preventing them from getting saved by causing them to feel sorry for themselves.

Imagine what Finney would have said about today's "poor

victims of sin"! Here we have presumably born-again saints of God, new creations in Christ, who supposedly can't keep away from any sin at all. Name the sin, no matter how vile, and you can find a dozen Christian magazine articles and another dozen Christian books explaining how actually that sin is fairly common among Christians and that only secular counseling methods really are any good against it.

One magazine we used to subscribe to was so blatant with its issue-after-issue articles on how Christians are falling into sin after sin that my wife and I began calling it the "Sin of the Month Club." None of the articles ever suggested that these sins were despicable and evil and that God hated them, either. Rather, the authors told us that our duty was to "understand" while the sinner "struggled" with his sin.

Struggle Theology
Let's talk for a minute about Struggle Theology. This is an incredibly creative device invented to explain why professing Christians fail to conquer their sins. Rather than considering the possibility that the habitual sinner was never really born again, or the likelihood that he needs stronger spiritual medicine than pop psychology, Struggle Theology teaches that none of us really ever conquers his sins. "We all are sinners, period," Struggle Theologians say. "Forget that stuff about being more than conquerors in Christ and all things being possible to him who believes. Don't start thinking you are better than other people. In fact, we'd like you to *concentrate* on other people. Don't think about Jesus if you can help it. Think instead about sinners who call themselves Christians. These are your real role models. Whatever they can't do, you can't do either."

If a Struggle Theologian can find *one* person who professes to be a Christian and also is failing to overcome the sin of habitual drunkenness, he considers that sufficient reason to tell *all* of us that drunkenness is a difficult problem requiring complex coping strategies and that there are "no simple answers" to this problem. If you try to point out that the Bible says drunkenness is a *sin,* not a disease, and that we are supposed to live above sin, the Struggle Theologian will accuse you of thinking you are better than other people and of being insensitive to the real problems others face. He may even go so far as to claim that when the church calls sin "sin" and expects sinners to change their ways, we are driving the poor victims of sin even farther from the "healing" that supposedly only occurs when we unconditionally accept them *and* their bad behavior.

A complete, quick victory over any sin is impossible, according to Struggle Theology, since sin is actually not sin, but a disease caused by poor self-esteem, genetic deficiencies, and outside environmental influences. We are not supposed to hate sin, but to *understand* it, which means understanding its causes (these never include the sinner's personal responsibility for the sin). Some measure of improvement is possible, but only after you have had hours of hand-holding sessions with a card-carrying Struggle Theologian. As one such counselor told a friend of mine, "It took you twenty years to develop this personality problem, and it will take you twenty years to overcome it." Real helpful and powerful stuff, isn't it?

What is this "struggling" they preach, and to what can I liken it? Try this: a necking party in the backseat of a car. When you see a couple holding each other tight they can be wrestling . . . or they can be cuddling. When a Christian claims to be struggling with sins that he never seems to conquer, it's because he can't quit embracing them long enough to thrust them away. We Christians are supposed to deal with sin at the point of a sword, not to "struggle" with it.

Eve "struggled" with Satan in the garden of Eden. She didn't just jump right in and eat the fruit the minute the snake appeared. Satan had to stroke her up and down with tempting suggestions before she ate the fruit. This kind of struggling is just a coy way of giving in to sin. You put up the appearance of a fight to fool onlookers into thinking you're a good person who is trying his best, when really you never intended to permanently reject that sin in the first place.

"When Temptation Comes You'll Give Right In!"

In the musical *My Fair Lady,* Eliza Doolittle's father is a rake and a reprobate who has lived with Eliza's mother for years without marrying her. He is also a habitual drunkard and loafer who lives by begging loans from his friends rather than by working. His philosophy of sin is summed up in his song:

> "The Lord above made liquor for temptation
> To see if man can turn away from sin.
> The Lord above made liquor for temptation, but . . .
>   With a little bit of luck
>   With a little bit of luck
> When temptation comes you'll give right in!"

By endorsing the idea of struggles without victory, the church today is sailing perilously close to Mr. Doolittle's position. By expecting nothing at all from the "poor sinners" we hug to our bosom, we actually encourage them to keep on sinning. This kind of "understanding" amounts to Satan's lie, "You shall not surely die."

Sin *is* addicting. The Bible says men can become slaves to it. But the Bible also says that you are responsible for your slavery if you do become a slave to any particular sin. Rather than excuse yourself, it is a reason to fear and dread that sin enough to flee to the blood of Jesus for deliverance.

Shape Up or Ship Out!

The Bible says that Christians are not slaves to sin. Paul wrote to the Romans:

> Don't you know that when you offer yourselves to someone to obey him as slaves, you are slaves to the one whom you obey—whether you are slaves to sin, which leads to death, or to obedience, which leads to righteousness? But thanks be to God that though you used to be slaves to sin, you wholeheartedly obeyed the form of teaching to which you were entrusted. You have been set free from sin and have become slaves to righteousness. (Romans 6:16-18)

Note that there are two distinct groups mentioned: those who are slaves to sin, and those who are slaves to righteousness. Each group has chosen its own master. Sin's slaves are headed for death. Since Christians are headed for life, not death, Christians are not slaves to sin. We used to be slaves to sin, but we have been set free. We are now slaves to righteousness.

Paul gave the Corinthians a list of sins that disqualify a person from even being considered a Christian:

> Do you not know that the wicked will not inherit the kingdom of God? Do not be deceived: Neither the sexually immoral nor idolaters nor adulterers nor male prostitutes nor homosexual offenders nor thieves nor the greedy nor drunkards nor slanderers nor swindlers will inherit the kingdom of God. (1 Corinthians 6:9, 10)

He gives another list of sins associated with depraved minds at the beginning of Romans:

> They are full of envy, murder, strife, deceit and malice. They are gossips, slanderers, God-haters, insolent, arrogant and boastful; they invent ways of doing evil; they disobey their parents; they are senseless, faithless, heartless, ruthless. Although they know God's righteous decree that those who do such things deserve death, they not only do these very things but also approve of those who practice them. (Romans 1:29)

Being trapped in any of the sins in either of these lists is incompatible with calling someone a Christian.

Someone who claims to be a Christian and at the same time claims that he cannot shake a particular sin is straddling the line. He is either a Christian who has discovered that having problems gets him attention, or a non-Christian actually trapped in a sin who is claiming to be a Christian. In either case, the medicine is the same: "Shape up or ship out!"

Paul told the Corinthians what to do with the "poor victim" of incest in their midst—a man who was cohabiting with his father's wife. The Corinthians were proud of the way they were unconditionally accepting this fellow. Paul wasn't proud of them for doing this, though! He said, "Shouldn't you rather have been filled with grief and have put out of your fellowship the man who did this?"

When confronted with the demand, "Shape up or ship out," the hypochondriac Christian's problems should quickly go away. After all, he's only trying to get attention. Once he realizes that in God's kingdom the *righteous* are supposed to get the attention, and that he is perfectly capable of being righteous, even "tough" sins suddenly lose their grip. Once a Christian starts fighting his sins, the devil *has* to flee!

When the non-Christian who desires Christian fellowship realizes that it's not enough to be the same old person struggling with the same old sins, and that he can be a *new* person who has the power of the Holy Spirit changing his life, he will be more likely to actually become a true Christian. When our preachers can spend less time counselling the supposedly saved, they will have more time to spend preaching to the definitely lost.

At the same time, the church has to start encouraging those who do right. Evangelism is for non-Christians. Nurture is for Christians. If the church lavished her care on her children, we would see more people wanting to get born-again into her family.

Satan knew he could do nothing with Adam and Eve as long as they were content with God and His gifts. So he tempted them with a false need for the tree of the knowledge of good and evil. Once our first parents became discontented with what God had given them they were vulnerable to more of Satan's lies. Still, they wouldn't cross the line and actually eat the fruit as long as they were afraid that they would die. By denying that they had anything to fear from God, Satan had them straddling the line. In the next chapter we'll see the device Satan used to pull them over the rest of the way . . . and that he uses on us today to neutralize our witness in the world.

3

In with the In-Crowd

I'm in with the in-crowd.
I go where the in-crowd goes.
I'm in with the in-crowd.
And I know what the in-crowd knows.

Fifties song

"You will not surely die," the serpent said to the woman. "For God knows that when you eat of it your eyes will be opened, and you will be like God, knowing good and evil."

Genesis 3:4, 5

A few days ago I was watching Al Menconi's video seminar, *Everything You Need to Know About Rock Music.* Now, I figure that I don't need to know much more than I know already about rock music. My own tastes veer more to folk and classical. But I was curious about why millions of kids today are so captivated by it, and thought perhaps Mr. Menconi had some answers.

The real surprise, as I watched this video, was to discover that *Christian* kids are flocking in droves to gobble up heavy metal rock, punk rock, dead rock, glam rock, and all the other tints and shades of deep purple sin purveyed by secular rock musicians. Having become a Christian shortly after college myself, I rather expected that other young Christians would react to secular music the same way I did—listen to the lyrics and trash any albums that preach sin. Yet here brother Menconi was having to spell the message out to Christian kids that no, you don't automatically soak up every musical message the world has to offer and yes, sometimes what's "in" can be bad, bad stuff.

Now, I'm not really off the latest boat from outer space. I have heard that Christian kids are having rough times spiritually, which is another way of saying that they aren't necessarily letting their little lights shine, shine, shine like they should. But it's another thing to see those fresh, innocent young things actually asking questions like, "What's the matter with listening to [a particular singer that teaches incest, suicide, and drug abuse]? He's so *cute!*" or watching them admit that some band that does simulated sex on stage is their "favorite group." The question I hoped to see answered was, "What's in it for these Christian kids? What is attracting them to this vile stuff?"

Fatal Attraction

What *is* so appealing about secular rock? Maybe it's the words. Rock songs have different messages, but the essence of what rock songs are saying is this:

- Sex is where it's at and the more the better, or
- Get violent; go wild, or
- Life is empty, you might as well kill yourself, or
- The only good Christian is a dead Christian, or
- Some combination of the above.

Most young Christian men and women will tell you (for obvious reasons) that they don't even listen to the words. But what do they love so much about this music then?

They may say they like the beat. But lots of music has a great beat. Marches have a great beat, but you don't see many young people getting off on John Philip Sousa. Christian rock has the same beat as secular rock, and you can even listen to the words without blushing. But a lot of Christian kids say Christian rock is boring.

Then what is the reason? Is it the sound? Christian rock has the same sound. Is it the classy way the performers dress? Or maybe their exemplary lives? Not likely.

Christian young people like secular rock because *the in-crowd in their school like secular rock.* When jazz was in, all the young people liked jazz. When swing became the rage, everyone was into swing. Now that heavy metal is in, all the kids just adore heavy metal. This has to be more than a coincidence.

Rock itself is probably not the issue. The fact that *other kids like rock* is the issue. Liking secular rock is one way of fitting in with the unbelievers. If tomorrow Prince and KISS are "out," all the Christian kids will suddenly discover that these rockers are baby stuff and the *new* "in" groups are the ones they really like. Peer pressure is the only explanation for this mass taste for whatever is popular.

My wife Mary remembers feeling the pressure when the Beatles made their debut. She was a little girl of seven and was the only girl in her class whose parents did not own a television and who never listened to the radio. All of a sudden everyone at school was talking about the Beatles. Mary instinctively knew that to admit that she didn't know what they were talking about would make her the butt of jokes for months.

Uncle Remus might have told the story this way:

Sis'tah Mary Meet de Beatles

De kids, dey all ravin' 'bout de Beatles.

Mary she lay low. Think mebbe de Beatles are singin' bugs.

Mary she hear mo' talk 'bout the Beatles bein' the greatest.

Mary she lay low. Mebbe she heared wrong and dey really "de Beagles." "Could dey be singin' dogs?" she wonders.

De Beatles still fill all de talk.

Mary she lissen roun' an' she lissen roun' an' she find out 'bout the Beatles.

Now Mary talk Beatles wi' all de others . . . but now what's all dis 'bout de Rollin' Stones?

Dare to Be a Spaniel?

Peer pressure rules in the schools. Whatever dress is in style, all the kids are wearing it, even if it's girls wearing boy's boxer underwear outside their slacks, or mohawk hairdos. If it's in for boys to carry their books under their arms and girls to carry them in front, or if it's the style to carry your books with a rubber book strap, that's how everyone carries them.

"Oh, well, that's just teenagers. Kids always want to fit in." Wait a minute here! Kids aren't the only subjects of peer pressure. Peer pressure rules in business, too. In most parts of the country the three-piece suit is the only acceptable uniform. At my computer job there was no formal dress code. Nevertheless the few nonconformists who refused to wear a suit jacket and tie felt the pressure to conform. One by one they either left the company or bought a tie.

Book straps and suit jackets are not really serious matters, of course. Peer pressure in the church is a different matter. Peer pressure has moved the church away from its Biblically-based values. No one thought about woman pastors until the feminist movement became vocal. No one even thought about letting a practicing homosexual be a member of a church, never mind its pastor, until the homosexuals came out of the closet in American society. Divorce for "any and every cause" was never coddled or even condoned in the church until divorce became rampant outside the church.

Whenever the church changes her mind on a doctrine, after centuries of commitment to it, right on the heels of a similar change in society at large, we can suspect that the change of doctrine has come from her desire to conform. Letting your doctrine slip under peer pressure from the world is flirting with the devil.

Peer pressure tries to tear you away from old allegiances and cement you firmly into the herd. Satan put the thumbscrews of peer pressure on Adam and Eve. Would they follow Satan, who was right there pressuring them, or God, who was not?

Satan pulled out all the stops in persuading Adam and Eve to join his club.

Divide and Conquer

Satan's first strategy was to weaken Adam and Eve's allegiance to God by claiming that God had lied to them. Satan was just setting the record straight and telling them the true situation. Adam and Eve were placed smack in the middle. Would they believe God or Satan?

If they stuck with God, they had to get rid of Satan. Do you know how hard it is to call someone a liar to his face? Have you ever been in a situation where you should have called someone out for a lie, but held your tongue? Then you know the temptation Adam and Eve were facing.

"I'm Only Trying to Help!"

Secondly, the devil used the "I am only trying to help" ploy. Adam and Eve had been deceived to their hurt, he claimed. Satan was only looking out for their interests! In fact, though, he was being a busybody, poking his nose in where it didn't belong.

The director of three state-licensed day-care centers in Missouri told me about the social workers who often visited her centers. Whenever she objected to the social workers' meddling, they said, "But we are only trying to help you." Translated this meant, "We are only trying to take over your day-care center."

Her answer always was, "Please don't 'help' me so much." Adam and Eve should have taken lessons from her.

The Glamor of Gossip

Next Satan offered Adam and Eve a choice bit of gossip. He knew why God wouldn't let them eat from the tree, and if they listened, he would let them in on the secret. They could "know what the in-crowd knows" if they listened to him.

Now they had a real tactical problem. Have you ever tried to shut down a gossip with his momentum up? You have to be downright rude:

"No, I don't want to hear it."

"Oh, but just let me tell you about . . . "

"Really, I don't want to hear it."

"But I just have to tell *someone*."

"You don't have to tell *me*."

"I can't believe you don't want to hear about Bob and Karen's divorce. Y'know they fight all the time; well . . . "

And you finally have to put your fingers in your ears, hum a little tune to drown out the noise, and run out of the room.

The Scorn Is as High as a Bird in the Sky . . .

While drawing Adam and Eve on with promises of help and hidden knowledge, Satan also drove them, on with scorn.

What do the other kids do when one of them takes a stand for what is right against the crowd? They make fun of him. When you won't take drugs, when you want to stay a virgin till you are married, when you won't go with the gang to steal lumber from the neighboring construction site, they mock you. The in-crowd laughed at John the Baptist. They laughed at Jesus. If you stand up for Jesus, they'll laugh at you, too.

Adam and Eve had already felt the sting of Satan's scorn when he answered Eve to this effect: "You don't really believe that, do you? My, you are a simpleton to take God at His word. You won't *really* die." They would certainly risk more of the same if they defended God further.

"Just Sign Here, Please"

The final temptation is the promise that you will become part of the in-crowd yourself. Satan promised them, "You will become like God knowing good and evil." He implied that he already was a member of the Like-God Club. God, the head of the club, was trying to keep the club too exclusive, but Satan knew the key to let them in. All they had to do was eat the forbidden fruit and they, like him, would be like God, knowing good and evil.

Satan didn't realize that God wasn't just like him. What he should have said is, "You will become like *me*, knowing evil as well as good." Adam and Eve already knew what was good—to obey God. What Satan offered them was intimate knowledge of evil from the sinner's point of view.

Could Adam and Eve have resisted the devil if they had known what to do? We'll never know, because they didn't try. Their hearts were already half convinced of their "need" for the tree of the knowledge of good and evil. Eve, by her own admission, was totally taken in by Satan and actually believed what Satan said. Adam wasn't deceived, but neither was he inclined to put up a big fight. He was flirting with the devil.

Be Ye Conformed to This World?

Satan and the world have always been anxious for us to fit in. Peter writes, "For you have spent enough time in the past doing what pagans choose to do—living in debauchery, lust, drunkenness, orgies, carousing, and detestable idolatry. They think it strange that you do not plunge with them into the same flood of dissipation, and they heap abuse on you" (1 Peter 4:3, 4). You know what I'm talking about. Aren't you constantly bombarded with temptations to fit in, to conform, to be like everyone else?

At my first job out of college, my co-workers warned me that everyone who was promoted had to throw a party and had to supply alcoholic beverages. This was peer pressure. Or take another example, common to most of us who have worked in the non-Christian business world. A bunch of the guys are making off-color speculations about the attractive new secretary. You know you should say something or leave, but you also know your protest would offend them. This too is peer pressure.

We protest: "I don't want to be an oddball." But who are the oddballs? Is this God's world or not? If this is God's world, ultimately those who fail to conform to His decrees will be the outsiders, not us. In the meantime, it's OK not to fit in. Elijah didn't fit in. John the Baptist didn't fit in. Jesus Himself didn't fit in. You just have to decide who you want to fit in with: Elijah, John, and Jesus, or the world.

We rationalize: "How can I witness to people if they won't even talk with me?" But few of the Pharisees would talk with Jesus either. In fact, they made fun of Him! Should the eternal Son of God have conformed to the Pharisees so he could talk to them?

Remember Nicodemus. The in-crowd may not talk to you in public, but if you're patient and stand firm, you will get your chance in private.

The Friends Justify the Means

The worst kind of peer pressure comes, not from the world, but from the pulpit, the Christian college lectern, and the Christian media. These people, especially professors and journalists, face incredible pressure to preach a conformist message—to try to fit in with respectable secular society. Joel Belz wrote in the June 6, 1988 edition of *World* magazine:

> The pressures are stern. I know that partly because I just participated in the annual convention of the Evangelical Press Association, a gathering of journalists and publishing personnel firmly committed to the authority of Scripture. This year, for professional purposes, we met jointly with people from the Associated Church Press—a much more liberal group with only a sprinkling of evangelically oriented members. Through the three days, I was impressed how often I was tempted to trim my own sails, to refrain from saying what I really believed, just so I could have the respect of those professional colleagues from the other end of the ideological spectrum. They just kept calling me to the middle of the road.

Joel Belz explained why journalists and college professors are the most tempted to compromise.

> Professors and writers, like all of us, have peers. Like all of us, they like to please their peers. The problem is that professors and writers work so exclusively in the world of ideas and values. To please their peers they have to do with those ideas what their peers find satisfactory. That whole process has a tendency to tug the ideas even of well-meaning people in the direction of the peer group.

When our Christian leaders make friends outside the church, they are tempted to make compromises to fit in with their new friends. This then filters into their message. They start telling us to act in a way that will reflect credit on them in the eyes of their unbelieving peers.

Some church leaders preach that in order to be witnesses in this world, we have to be respectable. We have to fit in and do what the world does, only ever so much more so. Rich people are looked up to in the world—so Christians must present a rich, prosperous image. Beauty and health are highly valued in the world—so Christians must be more beautiful and more fit than Jane Fonda.

Divorce is rampant in the world. Those who believe that Christians should fit in aren't concerned when large numbers of church members start divorcing. They say things like, "We shouldn't condemn anybody for divorcing, no matter what their reason. The Bible teachings on divorce are culturally determined, anyway. They applied to the Greek/Roman/Jewish/African/Near Eastern culture of Paul's time, but they don't apply today." As long as any sin is widely practiced by non-Christians, they can't bear to discourage it!

These leaders try to discourage us from separating from the world because they think Christians are supposed to be an advertisement for the church. The idea is to maximize profits (i.e., add the maximum number of new church members) by selling the product (church membership). Jesus told His hearers to count the cost before deciding to follow Him—these leaders want to disguise the cost, lest a new prospect for the product be lost. We shouldn't try to be different, they maintain, because people would be turned off if they thought they would have to change to become Christians. "Maybe we'll tell them after they join," they reason. "Sort of a new doctrine of the Second Blessing—first you get saved, then perhaps later you can think about being holy." Come to think of it though, if Christians look just like non-Christians, maybe we won't have to tell the new church members about holiness at all!

"We Are the World"

An even more subtle lie than that we should become like the world to win the world is the lie that Christians are *already* like the world. One poll said that Christian teenagers are just as involved in fornication, if not more so, as their non-Christian counterparts. (This may be true, but who says these lustful kids are *Christians?*) The Christian magazine Sin-of-the-Month Club stresses in almost every introduction to every article that Christians are no different from the world, and that we have every problem the world has, to the same degree if not more so.

Most writers of Typical Bad Evangelical Magazine articles intend to say, "Here is a horrible problem. A really horrible problem, which needs the immediate attention of the church. And here is how I or somebody whose work I admire says we should solve it."

The actual effect of articles like this is more like this: "Here is a sin. This is a sin which you never could get away with before in the church, only in the world. Now this sin is epidemic in the church and the church is doing nothing to the people who are doing it. In fact, if the church follows this article's suggestions, people who sin this sin will soon become a privileged class. I can commit that sin too and just blend in with everyone else, and they won't do anything to me either. And by the way, as long as we have become so like the world already, why should we draw the line at any other sin either?"

Unless you are preaching God's judgment, the only purpose served by showing how the church is like the world is to give the church an excuse to become more like the world.

Eve was not too bright when she fell for Satan's promise to get her into the in-crowd. She and Adam already were in the in-crowd. They walked and talked with God every day! Similarly, Christians (and Christian leaders) who today scramble to fit into the secular Left or the secular Right or the secular Up or the secular Down are all showing poor judgment. We Christians *are* the in-crowd! The world is supposed to want to join *us!*

Ah, but the worldly in-crowd has some delights to offer that often seem tempting at first sight. We'll be back in a minute with a look at this lure Satan uses to bait his hook.

4

If It Feels Good . . .

> *If it feels good, do it.*
>
> Bumper sticker
>
> *When the woman saw that the fruit of the tree was good for food and pleasing to the eye, and also desirable for gaining wisdom, she took some and ate it.*
>
> Genesis 3:6

Mrs. Jones had just baked a chocolate cake and the smell filled the house. Her son, Jim, had been suffering for an hour while the cake cooled. He was watching his mother frost the cake and looking like a starving beagle.

"I have to go put the laundry in the dryer. Don't touch the cake," his mother warned. "I am saving it for tonight's Bible study."

You know what's going to happen. You've read this story a hundred times before in Sunday school object lessons.

Jim sat and looked at the cake, savoring the aroma. His stomach began to growl. He decided to admire his mother's handiwork a little more closely. He checked out the near side. Then he turned the plate around and looked at the other side.

He noticed that the frosting on that side wasn't quite smooth. The knife had left a little ridge.

"Mom told me not to touch the cake," he reasoned, "but she really meant not to eat it. She couldn't have meant that I can't do some minor repairs."

He tried to smooth the ridge out with his finger. Of course he got some of the frosting on his finger, so he licked it off. Now he noticed that another spot in the frosting wasn't quite smooth, and encouraged by his first success (and likely by his taste of the frosting), he "repaired" that spot, too. As will happen, that little taste of frosting just made Jim feel even hungrier than he was before.

He thought, "Surely Mom wouldn't want me to be so hungry that I get sick, and I will get a piece of cake tonight anyway. I could take my piece now, and that wouldn't make any difference."

So Jim cut himself a piece, and just as he started to take his first bite, his mother caught him!

What was wrong with Jim's reasoning? Surely any reasonable person would agree with what he did, right? But mothers aren't always "reasonable" and Jim was confined to his room alone till supper, without his cake. All the rationalizations in the world didn't change his mother's decree that he shouldn't touch the cake.

Eve the Scientist

Once Eve had become convinced that she wanted to eat the forbidden fruit, she had to rationalize her disobedience. She adopted a scientific attitude toward the fruit. "I will examine the fruit, and if it seems good I will assume it is wholesome." She determined:

1) The fruit was good to eat,
2) The fruit was nice to look at, and
3) The fruit would make them wiser.

On the basis of this good outcome, she took the fruit and ate it.

This is the first case of a person using pseudo-science to overrule God's revelation. "I don't see anything wrong with it, therefore there is nothing wrong with it." This philosophy has been popularized as, "If it feels good, it is good," or "If it feels good, do it."

You can see Eve's presuppositions distorting her scientific objectivity. Eve couldn't tell for sure that the fruit was good to eat until she actually ate it. She could see that the fruit looked pretty, but what is pretty to you may not be pretty to me. How did she know the fruit would make them wise? The serpent, of course. She fell for his pitch hook, line, and sinker. So one observation was spurious, the second subjective, and the last based on hearsay.

Human psychology, the "scientific" basis for the "if it feels good, it is good" philosophy, falls down the same way. The desired result controls the experiment. Take sex outside of marriage for an example. Here is how a study on human sexuality may "discover":

1) Sex is a good thing,
2) Sex is pleasurable, and
3) Sex makes people more relaxed and therefore saner.

First, just as Eve assumed the fruit was good to eat before she tasted it, the clinician probably started the experiment believing that sex is a good thing, so that can hardly be called a conclusion. Second, what is pleasurable for one person may not be for another, so the second conclusion is based on subjective data. The third conclusion is based on the testimony of the people involved in the experiment, i.e. hearsay evidence, testimony which may be influenced by the way the psychologist asks his questions or his obvious desire for certain answers. Humanistic scientists, on the basis of this reasoning, would probably conclude that sex is "good" for everyone regardless of marital status.

Whether we're talking about Eve or my hypothetical psychologist, their experiments had nothing to do with reality. It doesn't matter whether the fruit is good to eat or not if God says we shouldn't eat it. It doesn't matter if sex is pleasurable outside of marriage if God forbids it.

The world doesn't consult God when it makes its scientific pronouncements. We Christians have to have a higher perspective.

The Lust of the Flesh, the Lust of the Eyes, and the Pride of Life

The Apostle John summarizes the world's perspective when he writes:

> Love not the world, neither the things that are in the world. If any man love the world, the love of the Father is not in him. For all that is in the world, the lust of the flesh, and the lust of the eyes, and the pride of life, is not of the Father, but is of the world. (1 John 2:15-16 KJV)

Maybe John had Eve in mind when he wrote this, because it exactly parallels her analysis of the fruit. She saw that the fruit was good for food—the lust of the flesh. She saw that it was pleasing to the eye—the lust of the eye. And she saw that it was desirable for gaining wisdom—the pride of life.

The *lust of the flesh* is our normal fleshly yearnings allowed to run wild. It's not wrong to be hungry, but when our diet takes over our lives, as in the case of the gourmet who lives his life for a new taste, or the compulsive dieter whose whole conversation centers on what she isn't eating this week, then normal desire has passed to lust. Our normal sexual desire, if left unchecked, will take over our minds and become lust. The desire for comfort and rest has become a lust when we turn our backs on the opportunities God gives us to minister because of possible danger or inconvenience.

You can see the *lust of the eyes* at work in a toddler:

- I see it
- It's pretty
- I want it
- I grab for it

and usually:

- I get it in my mouth
- I choke on it

The lust of the eyes works just the same way for adults with a little more rationalization and cover-up. We grab for things we see and want on our own terms, in our own timing, without consulting God.

Pride of life is trying to get ahead on our own terms. We Christians can fool ourselves into thinking we are serving God when we are really serving our own ambitions. We take a godly goal; for example, evangelizing the neighborhood of our church. We then reason that since God wants us to evangelize and since he wants all men to be saved and come to a knowledge of the truth, the important thing is to get people to where they can hear the message. From there anything goes. You can have an evangelistic car wash, or evangelistic casino night, or an evangelistic wine-tasting party, just so that you get people into the church to hear the message. Really the youth group wanted to have a car wash, but you tacked on evangelism. The ladies' auxiliary wanted a casino night to raise money for new pew cushions, but the board was a little uneasy about the gambling motif. A little homily in the middle of the evening was just the thing to sanctify the event.

"I Did It All for the Blimp"

The fifties movie *The Gospel Blimp* contains a good example of the pride of life leading Christians into sin. One night the members of a home Bible study started discussing ways to evangelize their host's neighbor, an obvious pagan in their eyes since he drank beer. They decided the easiest way to get out the message was to buy a blimp and pull a Bible message behind it over the whole town. If that didn't work they could drop tracts, concentrating their efforts on the neighbor's house.

So they did. They stepped out in faith, bought a tract of prime land outside of town for the hangar, then waited for the donations to start coming. Donations did roll in, including the most important donation, a used blimp. Sure now that God was with them, they named their group "International Gospel Blimps."

The "ministry" grew. One of their members quit work and

started giving full time to the blimp. The board of directors started calling him The Commander. They bought him a uniform and he became the figurehead of the operation.

In order to keep up the image of the ministry, the Commander had to make some "sacrifices." He moved into a new mansion and bought a jazzy car. His time with his family also got axed for the sake of the blimp. Now he was spending a lot of time out of town away from them speaking at conferences. The film shows him leaving on one of these trips, packing his golf clubs into the car and driving off, leaving his lonely and forlorn family behind.

You see what was happening. The Commander was starting to get ambitious. He spent money on a nice house for himself, for the sake of the blimp. He went to conferences where he was the big-shot speaker and got to have fun playing golf, for the sake of the blimp. In short, he was doing what he wanted to do and excusing it, because it was all for the blimp.

"If You Want It, Here It Is . . ."

The lust of the eyes, the lust of the flesh, and the pride of life all lead us to promote wants into needs and rationalize sinful attempts to grab what we want. But rationalization is not new. Men, women, and itty-bitty babies have been rationalizing their sins since Eden. What is new is that people can now get sympathy through Christian books, from the church, and even from the pulpit for desiring what God hasn't allowed them to have.

The same egalitarian spirit that has taken over our country has invaded the church. The reasoning goes like this: If you have it, I ought to have it too. The *desire* for something becomes the *right* to it.

Take the fictional example of Fred, for example. Fred was divorced three times, but now has been living on an even keel for some time, and he wants to go to seminary and study to be a pastor. When the denominational seminary won't accept him because of his past, the divorced members of the church rally around him and prevail on the church board to protest to the denomination's seminary committee. "How dare they reject any man who feels called to the ministry?" they fume. The seminary committee instructs the seminary not to cause a stink about it, but to let him in. The *desire* to be a minister gives Fred the *right* to study to be a minister, even though he was not a one-woman man, and therefore wasn't Biblically qualified. (See 1 Timothy 3:2.)

Should a man steal to feed his hungry family? Proverbs 6:30 says, "Men do not despise a thief if he steals to satisfy his hunger when he is starving." Therefore, the desperate need for food justifies stealing it, especially if everyone else has food, right? Modern ethics would utter a hearty, "Amen!" but Proverbs 6:30-31 says, "If he is caught, he must pay sevenfold, though it costs him all the wealth of his house."

People now consider it unfair if other people have happy marriages and they don't. A happy marriage is certainly worth having, but does it justify a person remarrying over and over till he gets it right? Apparently so, according to those who consult their own wishes more than they consult the Bible. Someone told my wife, Mary, the story of a woman whose husband had become incapacitated. Friends counselled the wife, "You're a young woman. You can't spend your whole life nursing a sick husband. You have your own needs to consider, too. Put him in a nursing home and get a divorce." What alarmed Mary was not the story, but that the woman who told her the story saw nothing wrong with it. Mary only got that woman to see the point by getting her to imagine how *she* would feel if she were incapacitated and her husband divorced *her*.

Things That Last

The whole problem with the "If it feels good, do it" philosophy is a problem of perspective. We so often look at things through the eyes of the world and don't try to see them the way God does. Worldly men look at the world through blinders. They miss out entirely on the big picture because they only care about how things affect them. They don't care about the future effects of their actions, or if what they do will last, because they live entirely for today.

John says of the lust of the flesh, the lust of the eyes, and the pride of life, "The world and its desires pass away, but the man who does the will of God lives forever" (1 John 3:17). Missing out on the chance to live forever so we can waste our time instead on things that are going to pass away is foolish. We should spend our effort on the things that last.

Playground or Battleground?

But gaining that perspective is hard, when the church encourages us to waste our time *playing*. A. W. Tozer, a Christian and Missionary Alliance preacher from 1919 to 1963, observed in one of his essays (from *The Best of A. W. Tozer*, Baker Book House, 1978, a book well worth having in your library):

> In the early days, when Christianity exercised a dominant influence over American thinking, men conceived the world to be a battleground. Our fathers believed in sin and the devil and hell as constituting one force; and they believed in God and righteousness and heaven as the other. These were opposed to each other in the nature of them forever in deep, grave, irreconcilable hostility. Man, so our fathers held, had to choose sides; he could not be neutral. For him it must be life or death, heaven or hell, and if he chose to come out on God's side he could expect open war with God's enemies. The fight would be real and deadly and would last as long as life continued here below. Men looked forward to heaven as a return from the wars, a laying down of the sword to enjoy in peace the home prepared for them. . . .
>
> How different today: the fact remains the same but the interpretation has changed completely. Men think of the world, not as a battleground but as a playground. We are not here to fight, we are here to frolic. We are not in a foreign land, we are at home. We are not getting ready to live, we are already living, and the best we can do is to rid ourselves of our inhibitions and our frustrations and live this life to the full. . . .
>
> That this world is a playground instead of a battleground has now been accepted in practice by the vast majority of evangelical Christians. They might hedge around the question if they were asked bluntly to declare their position, but their conduct gives them away. They are facing both

ways, enjoying Christ and the world too, and gleefully telling everyone that accepting Jesus does not require them to give up their fun, and that Christianity is just the jolliest thing imaginable.

Eve, as Tozer would have pointed out, couldn't have her fruit and eat it, too. We can't live both for the temporary things of this world and for Jesus.

How can you tell if you're living like a soldier of Christ or a playboy? Tozer gave a list of suggestions for self-examination in his essay entitled "Marks of the Spiritual Man" (also included in that excellent little book). His list includes

- The desire to be holy
- Wanting to see the honor of God advanced even at our own expense
- Wanting to carry your cross (now, how often have you heard *that* message lately?)
- Seeing life from God's viewpoint
- The desire to die right rather than to live wrong
- The desire to see others advance even at our own expense
- Making eternity-judgments rather than here-and-now judgments.

Notice how much of Tozer's list is occupied with our attitude towards the temporary things of this world. Health, wealth, fame, success, pleasure, and so on can become our goals, or we can have a spiritual perspective and see them merely as tools for serving God.

"It's My Party and I'll Fry If I Want To"

The question is, "Would you lay your tools down gladly if God called upon you to do so?" If you just can't bear to give it up, then the "tool" has become an idol.

Take a house, for instance. Owning your very own house is part of the American Dream, and when my parents were young, almost every family could do it. But owning a house is no longer something a family can take for granted. The wrong way to approach buying a house is this:

1) We want a house, so let's set buying a house as our goal.

2) We do not have enough income right now to buy a house and we are not saving any money.

3) Wife, you will get an outside job and we will save your income toward the down payment and use your income to meet the higher payments after that. We will cut back on all extras, which means no home-schooling curriculum. Besides, with Mommy at work, she can't home school anyway. Private Christian school is also out; too expensive. So all you older kids will go to public school, and you younger ones will be in daycare.

4) Now let's pray and ask God's blessing on our decision.

In contrast, the Christian way to approach buying a house is this:

1) Do we need a house to carry on our work?

   a) Is our family outgrowing the place we live in now or is the landlord threatening to put us out? Is there no one who owns an adequate place who will rent to our family? If there is someone, is the price he is asking almost as much as a house payment? Or,

   b) Is God leading us to do work—such as picking drunks off the streets, or taking in refugee families—that requires we own our own place?

2) Let's pray that God:

   a) Find us a place, and

   b) Provide the means to buy it.

3) Now we wait and keep our eyes open!

The wrong way first sets its desires on something in the world, then connives to get it. God may or may not be consulted as an afterthought. This is what Adam and Eve did. Since what they wanted was within their reach, they grabbed it.

The Christian way looks on worldly things as tools. When the family discovers that they need a new tool, they pray to God to provide it. When God provides it they say, "Thank You!" If God takes it back through theft or disaster, that's His business. If our first parents had consulted God first before eating the fruit, mankind wouldn't be in the mess we're in.

Someone may protest: "This sounds a little austere. Doesn't Paul say to Timothy, '[God] richly provides us with everything for our enjoyment'" (1 Timothy 6:17)? Yes, He does. But this verse and the ones following are directed to rich men who are told to use their riches as tools—to benefit others and to amass heavenly treasure. God wants us to enjoy what He gives us, but we should enjoy it like a carpenter enjoys his new hammer, not like a drunkard enjoys his wine.

As Tozer pointed out in another essay, "However jolly we Christians may become, the devil is not fooling." We can, and possibly may, party ourselves to death. While the world goes merrily marching on to the brave new homosexual-feminist-Socialist-New Age order, don't we have something more important to do than organize church picnics? When we've won the battle for America, *then* we can picnic!

Speaking of winning the spiritual battle of our day, we've got a little problem. Who's going to lead the troops? And in which direction? Stay tuned for an update on how Adam became the first Wrong-Way Corrigan, and how following his example today Christian husbands, parents, elders, and others in authority are unwittingly flying in the wrong direction.

5

Hot Crossed Roles

"You *decide, honey.*"
Dagwood Bumstead

When the woman saw that the fruit was good for food and pleasing to the eye, and also desirable for gaining wisdom, she took some and ate it. She also gave some to her husband, who was with her, and he ate it.
Genesis 3:1-6

"For crying out loud, Jay Nathanson thought. *What's he up to now?*

"Nathanson abruptly turned off the tape player and nosed his burgundy-red Ford into the parking lot. Stunned, he tried not to stare at the senior managers waving placards outside the Vatex Corp. plant. *It's a picket line, for Pete's sake. Jerry Gordé and his buddies have set up a picket line!*

"Nathanson parked, then stayed in the car for a moment to figure his next move. No way would he join that line—assuming that's what Gordé wanted. No. He'd just walk right past it and go to work. Grim-faced, he got out of the car, put his head down, and strode on into the building.

"Once inside, he shuffled a few papers. But he was too distraught to work. He wandered back out, saw a friend sitting in her car watching the picketing, got in. Together they commiserated. Suppose a customer drove up! And what about production? Nathanson was one of Vatex's top salespeople, and was only too well aware that the Richmond, Va., company was entering its busy season. But today the workers weren't going into the plant; they were staying outside, yukking it up with Gordé.

"*This is total insanity,* he thought ruefully. *Who would ever believe it? A CEO picketing his own company."*

The whole idea of a chief executive officer (CEO) picketing his own company *is* absurd. Why should the head of a company go on strike? If he doesn't like the way things are, all he needs to do is change them.

If something like this ever happened in the business world it would be worth a feature article in a business magazine. And that's what *Inc.* magazine gave it. The quote at the head of this chapter came (slightly cleaned up) from an article titled "Chairman Jerry's Cultural Revolution" in the August 1987 issue of *Inc.*

Satan likes to work through the boss when he can, as he did through Hitler and Stalin. Working through the boss is efficient. But sometimes the people in authority are on God's side and are difficult or impossible for Satan to work with. Then Satan takes a different tack. He stirs up rebellion among the followers, knowing that most of the time rulers would rather compromise than fight.

Satan can move the head by wagging the tail. He chose this strategy in the very beginning when dealing with Adam and Eve.

Were There Roles in the Garden?

But before we can talk about Satan's strategy of undermining the leader's authority, we need to prove that there *is* such a thing as proper authority.

Some people have said that there were no role distinctions in the garden of Eden. They say that role distinctions came after the Fall as part of the curse God placed on the woman.

The Order of Creation. This is not the Apostle Paul's interpretation! Paul tells Timothy that one reason why he did not permit a woman to teach or have authority over a man was that "Adam was formed first, then Eve" (1 Timothy 2:12). The Fall didn't change that!

In his teaching about head coverings, Paul reasons again from the order of creation. "For man did not come from woman, but woman from man, neither was man created for woman, but woman for man" (1 Corinthians 11:8). In other words, man was created before woman for a *reason.*

Other Clues in Genesis. There are other clues to Adam's headship in the Genesis story:

1) Adam was created first and alone.

2) Eve was created to be a help suitable for Adam, though Adam was never called a help for Eve.

3) Later, after Adam and Eve sinned, God addressed Adam first even though Eve was the principal speaker in their dealings with Satan.

The Head Names Those Under Him. In the Bible, the leader always names those he is head over, not the other way around. Thus God renamed Abram, Sarai, and Jacob to Abraham, Sarah, and Israel. Nebuchadnezzar changed Mattaniah's name to Zedekiah. Zechariah, father of John the Baptist, had final say over his son's name. Adam, who God placed over all creatures in creation, showed his headship when he named all the animals. Adam also named woman *ishah* "because she was taken out of *ish* [man]." The very word "woman" in the Hebrew is a derivative of "man," just as it is in English, because man was created first. Finally, Adam gave the first woman her personal name, Eve.

Have All the Roles Gone Stale?

Some people also say that there all role distinctions have been removed, since the sacrifice of Jesus. They quote Galatians

3:28, "There is neither Jew nor Greek, slave nor free, male nor female, for you are all one in Christ Jesus," and claim that this verse erases all role distinctions. They reason that you cannot have role distinctions among people who are all one.

But Paul, the author of Galatians, recognizes role distinctions in his other letters! In his letters to the Ephesians and Colossians, Paul explains how husbands and wives, children and parents, and slaves and masters should behave in their roles. When Paul wrote to Philemon, the master of Onesimus, about how Philemon should deal with Onesimus now that this runaway slave was returning home, he didn't argue on the basis of "There is neither slave nor free, for they are all one in Christ Jesus," but pleaded with Philemon as "Paul the old man" asking a favor.

Yet others, recognizing that Paul did teach about roles, still try to eliminate at least some Scriptural roles. They say, "Yes, Paul does set role distinctions for households. Galatians 3:28 is not referring to households; it is referring to the church. Paul never meant for us to make role distinctions *in the church* on the basis of ethnic background, economic status, or sex. Therefore we will let this verse override the verses about elders being the husbands of just one wife, and ordain women."

But nothing in the context of this verse lets us wipe out role qualifications in the church, either. The discussion surrounding this verse deals with the question, "Do Jews and Gentiles get saved differently? Do Jews get saved through the law, and Gentiles through faith?" Paul's answer is, "You are all sons of God through faith in Christ Jesus, for all of you who were baptized into Christ have clothed yourselves with Christ" (Galatians 3:26, 27). Then he says, "There is neither Jew nor Greek," etc. There are no different kinds of salvation for Jews or Greeks, male or female, slave or free. We have all became part of the same church in the same way.

This verse is talking about salvation, not roles. We have to look elsewhere in the New Testament to see what it says about church roles.

Heads Will Role

In any role relationship some person or group of people leads and the rest follow. Even in a business partnership there is usually a senior partner. When the Bible describes the duty of a follower it uses words like *obey, submit,* and *respect.* Wherever you see these words used in the Bible, that's a role relationship.

In the home, wives are supposed to submit to their husbands, children to their parents, and slaves to their masters (Ephesians 5:22, 6:1, 6:5). We are all supposed to submit to the ruling authorities in the state and pay our taxes to support their work (Romans 13:1-6). And in the church the Bible tells us to give the elders double honor or, as one of my seminary professors said, *honor* and *honorarium*—respect and financial support (1 Timothy 5:17).

But what about the flip side of the coin? What is the head's responsibility? Why, obviously he is supposed to lead the others! But does he lead like Benito Mussolini, Casper Milquetoast, or something in between? The following chart shows the possibilities:

	− NURTURE +	
A U T H O R I T Y +	STONEWALL serves nobody	THE PATSY role reversal
	TYRANNOSAUR serves himself	GOOD LEADER servant and leader

Leading means taking authority over those you lead, but it also means taking care of them. The diagram shows authority (from lenient to totalitarian) on the left and nurture (from low to high) on the top.

Low authority and low nurture gives you Stonewall Backsoon. Stonewall's philosophy is, "Don't bother me with any problems, and if you do, I'll get back to you tomorrow." Needless to say, "tomorrow" never comes. This breed of leader can be found most often in a soft easy chair behind a newspaper.

High authority and low nurture produces Tyrannosaurus Max. Max has a pretty fierce bark and often a savage bite. He says, "He governs best who is a beast. You can do anything you want as long as it's what I told you to do."

Low authority and high nurture produces a pathetic character, the Patsy. Old Patsy's dearest wish is to grow up someday to be a big strong boy like his mother, or wife, or daughter. His motto is, "Yes, dear." The least opposition causes Patsy to wilt. He really *wants* to help—in fact, he'll stay up all night holding hands and crying with you when you have problems—but he just can't force himself to play the heavy by taking any unpopular stand.

The good leader is both high on authority and high on nurture. He knows he is responsible to God for what happens under his jurisdiction and therefore takes his authority seriously. But he also cares for his flock like a good shepherd.

The fashion has swung in America from one extreme to the other. During the First Great Awakening pastors gained significant influence in America because they were good leaders. Their influence lasted for more than a hundred years. But later many pastors abused their authority, adding heavy burdens to Jesus' easy yoke. They became tyrants and the flock rebelled.

Modern pastors exert very little authority in the flock. A. W. Tozer explains it this way in his essay, "The Responsibility of Leadership":

> The poor conditions of the churches today may be traced straight to their leaders. When, as sometimes happens, the members of a local church rise up and turn their pastor out for preaching the truth, they are still following a leader. Be-

hind their act is sure to be found a carnal (and often well-to-do) deacon or elder who usurps the right to determine who the pastor shall be and what he shall say twice each Sunday. In such cases the pastor is unable to lead the flock. He merely *works* for the leader; a pitiful situation indeed.

I have seen pastors who were told by a worship committee what they would preach on Sunday morning. I have seen pastors driven from their churches because their preaching became too pointed. I have seen pastors who won't make any decision without forming a committee to study the question first. Many modern pastors have become Patsies.

Giving Honor Unto the Wife as Unto the Stronger Vessel

If modern pastors have become Patsies, modern husbands have become Stonewall Backsoons or Tyrannosaurus Maximums. S.B.s generally congregate in the cities. T.M.'s can be found anywhere. What they have in common is that both treat their wives as if the wife were the stronger vessel.

Peter tells husbands to "be considerate as you live with your wives and treat them with respect as the weaker partner (or the weaker *vessel*—KJV)" (1 Peter 3:7). A vessel is a container or a dish. You don't let the children use the fine china at mealtime. And you don't use a Ming vase for a flowerpot! Having respect for the weaker dishes means you give them special handling and protection. Peter tells husbands to honor their wives by giving them that same kind of consideration and protection.

Modern men say to women, "We are going to honor you by removing your protection. We are going to honor you by pretending you are tough." A prime example of this is the divorce laws, which now "honor" wives whose husbands unilaterally decide to back out of their marriage covenant by throwing the wives (and their children) out into the world penniless. "Modern women are tough and independent," legislators rationalize. "They can handle it."

This is just the way Adam treated Eve in the garden. He was about as much use to her as a wall when she had her conversation with the devil.

"You Decide, Honey"

Satan should by rights have addressed his questions to Adam. But since Satan chose to deal directly with Eve, she should have said, "Here is my husband. He heard the command directly from God. Discuss this with him." When Eve did not defer to Adam, who according to the text was "with her," Adam should have taken control.

What Adam did instead was something men have been doing to their wives ever since. He waited to see how things would come out!

One of our readers wrote us a letter complaining about the kind of child-rearing where parents take all of the credit if their kids turn out right and none of the blame if they turn out wrong. She called it "no-fault, only-credit child-rearing." Well, Adam was engaging in "no-fault, only credit husbanding"! He sat back and let Eve do the talking and decision-making. If the decision turned out right, he would have the satisfaction of having participated in the decision. If things went wrong, he wouldn't be to blame. He would just blame the decision on Eve.

We men still do this.

Our wife asks, "Where should we go for dinner?"

We say, "Oh, honey, you decide."

So she suggests a place. If it's all right with us we agree. If we have strong objections we let her know and she comes up with another.

Now we've agreed on the place she chose and we go there. We wait a half hour for our table. The soup is watery. The steak is almost all burnt to a cinder and the places which aren't rival a boot sole for durability. Your wife's lobster is undercooked and the waiter is surly about taking it back to be heated some more. They are out of every dessert on the menu you want and when you settle on a bowl of vanilla ice cream just to have something, it arrives melted.

Who is to blame? Your wife is, of course! *She* chose the place, so when you leave and she starts to complain about the evening, you say, "I had a bad feeling about this place as soon as you mentioned it, but you had your heart so set on going here, I just didn't want to disappoint you." Or if you are the more irascible sort, you lay into her for choosing such a crummy place to come to eat.

Many an all-out rhubarb has started this way. Your wife knows that you had the right to overrule her if you had wanted to, and resents you placing the blame on her. You, in turn, refuse to take any blame at all for the fiasco that resulted.

Many times the decision is much more serious than where you will eat supper.

She: Should we home school the kids?

He: Do what you want, dear.

She (months later): Boy, I am burned out.

He: I didn't think it was such a good idea at the time.

(Successful home schooling needs the commitment of both parents, even if the father is only the rooting gallery for the mother.) Or . . .

She: Should we have another baby?

He: You take care of them. It's your decision.

Later, when the kids grow up and discipline becomes a real problem for Mom, Dad says, "It was your decision to have them in the first place." Many a cad has even divorced his wife for having one too many children when he said it was "her decision."

The whole future of mankind rested on what Adam decided in the garden of Eden, but his silence said, "Eve, you decide." When God confronted him, he said, "The woman You put here with me—she gave me some fruit from the tree, and I ate it. Eve made the decision; I'm not responsible."

Roling Under the Rug

Church leaders do the same thing. A feminist woman comes and demands the right to be a pastor: "Let the little woman have her way."

Practicing homosexuals resent being excluded from the church: "They are people made in the image of God. How can we exclude them from membership in the church? Let them come."

Church leaders seem to have forgotten that their main loyalty is to God, to protect the purity of His church. God's Word says that one of the qualifications of an elder (and pastors are elders) is that he must be a one-woman man (1 Timothy 3:2, Titus 1:6). A woman can't have this qualification. God Himself excludes homosexual offenders from His kingdom (1 Corinthians 6:9); therefore, we are right not to let them join His church.

The Presbyterian Church is a good example of what can happen when the leaders of the church are "compassionate" or indecisive when they should exercise authority. Modernism, or theological liberalism, had swept all Europe and had invaded many of the American seminaries, including Harvard, Yale, and Princeton. The Northern Presbyterian church was still largely controlled by the conservatives, but an ever-increasing number of new, young ministers were embracing liberalism.

The conservatives did not react to liberalism by swiftly ejecting any minister who embraced it. Instead, three times (in 1910, 1916, and 1923) they passed a proposal that the denomination affirm "The Five Fundamentals" of Christian faith. As long as the church's official position was OK, they thought they had done their duty in protecting the flock.

The liberal ministers in their turn drafted a document in 1923 called the *Auburn Affirmation* stating their views and started gathering signatures in support of it. A small minority of 150 ministers brought it to the next General Assembly. By the end of that year, over 1300 ministers had signed it. Nothing was done to the people promoting this challenge to Biblical Christian doctrine. Three years later, the liberals gained control of the entire denomination. A decade or so later, they threw out the conservative leaders.

What was the result of the conservatives' compassionately allowing the liberals to remain in the denomination? The conservatives were ejected and the whole Northern Presbyterian denomination including its seminaries was left in the liberals' control. The denomination owned the seminaries, the pastors' pension fund, and most of the church buildings. The conservative ministers were dumped out basically penniless. They had lost their congregations and everything they had put away for their retirement. The congregations who tried to secede from the denomination had to fight in court to retain their church buildings. The conservative congregations who remained in the denomination, many of them ignorant of what had happened, just scratched their heads and wondered why the preaching wasn't quite the same anymore.

The conservatives could have saved the Presbyterian denomination if they had taken their roles as the heads of God's church seriously. If they had ejected the liberal pastors when they first appeared instead of humoring them, they could have held the line against liberalism. Then the liberals would have had to start the new churches and invest in the new church buildings and leave their pensions behind for their newfound beliefs.

When the Presbyterian ministers of the late 1800s and early 1900s stand at God's judgment seat, what will they say? "We couldn't discipline so many young men for a thing like liberalism. Besides, liberalism came in like a flood and simply washed us away. There was nothing we could do." Just what Adam tried to say to God in the garden of Eden.

"There Was Nothing I Could Do"

That is what we all say when what we really mean is, "I didn't do what I should have done because I didn't want to, or it was too hard, or it was too unpopular." Adam said, "Eve ate the fruit first, and there was nothing I could do but follow her lead." "There was nothing we could do, and therefore, we are not responsible for the bad result."

But God doesn't buy it. When God puts someone in charge of a household, a church, a government, or the garden of Eden, he expects him to exercise all the authority of their position for Him. The head is responsible even for his decision to abide by someone else's decision. Thus, even though Eve had the conversation with the serpent, and Eve was the first person to eat the forbidden fruit, Adam was held responsible for the sin (Romans 5:12-21). Likewise, husbands are responsible before God for everything they do or allow others to do in their households. Church leaders are responsible before God for everything they do or allow others to do in their flock. And rulers are responsible for everything they do or allow others to do under their jurisdiction.

What the head does has repercussions for everything under his headship. When Adam sinned, all of us and all creation came under bondage (1 Corinthians 15:22, Romans 1:18-21). As many have noted, the whole household of a drunkard feels the burden of his sin. Proverbs 29:2 says, "When the righteous thrive, the people rejoice; when the wicked rule, the people groan," and verse 12 says, "If a ruler listens to lies, all his officials become wicked."

A. W. Tozer observed the same thing about the kings of Israel. He said:

> Whatever sort of man the king turned out to be, the people were soon following his leadership. They followed David in the worship of Jehovah, Solomon in the building of the Temple, Jeroboam in the making of a calf and Hezekiah in the restoration of the Temple worship.

As goes the king, so goes the people.

By destroying or corrupting a ruler Satan can pervert whole masses of people. That is why he attacked Adam. As we have so painfully experienced recently, when a Christian leader falls publicly, the whole church is embarrassed. The next section shows Satan's dealings with one *very* prominent Christian leader, Jesus Christ Himself, and how Jesus countered his attack.

PART TWO

In the Wilderness

Then Jesus was led by the Spirit into the desert to be tempted by the devil. . . .

Matthew 4:1

6

Flirting with Pleasure

Though the fig tree does not bud and there are no grapes on the vines, though the olive crop fails and the fields produce no food, though there are no sheep in the pen and no cattle in the stalls, yet will I rejoice in the LORD, I will be joyful in God my Savior.

Habakkuk 3:17, 18

Then Jesus was led by the Spirit into the desert to be tempted by the devil. After fasting forty days and forty nights, he was hungry. The tempter came to him and said, "If you are the Son of God, tell these stones to become bread."

Jesus answered, "It is written: 'Man does not live on bread alone, but on every word that comes from the mouth of God.' "

Matthew 4:1-4

Little snowballs into mighty avalanches grow. A tiny crack in the dike can lead to a breach that floods the countryside. It only takes one spark to start a raging forest fire.

Satan knows this, and that is why he is always trying to pry the church off her firm foundation on the rock. Just one little weakness here and another crack there, and he knows he can get our whole building to sag.

Satan may roam around like a roaring lion, but when attacking the church he first appears as a tiny termite taking tiny nibbles in the beams. He has a strategy, an order of temptation. This is wise of him, because if he first approached us with the threat, "Deny Christ or else!" most of us would know enough to just say no. Instead, Satan tries to lead us from one "small" compromise to another. But these compromises are not chosen at random. They have a definite sequence, and we can know what it is.

The Order of Temptation

The Bible says that Jesus was "tempted in every way just as we are" (Hebrews 4:15). We are not left in the dark as to *how* exactly Jesus was tempted, either. Both Luke and Matthew record the epic encounter between Jesus and Satan when Jesus was led into the wilderness to be tempted.

The accounts in Luke 4 and Matthew 4 differ only in the order of the temptations. Both show the temptation to turn stones into bread first. The temptation to jump off the Temple is listed second in Matthew, but third in Luke. However, Matthew also tells us that the temptation to rule the kingdoms of the earth by bowing down to Satan was followed by Jesus renouncing Satan and Satan leaving. Matthew also uses "time-words" such as *then* and *again,* whereas Luke merely lists the temptations without any chronology. So we can be sure that the Matthew account provides the exact order of these temptations:

- First, the temptation to turn stones into bread.
- Second, the temptation to jump off the Temple.
- Third, the temptation to rule the kingdoms of men.

This section will explain what each of these temptations mean, how and why they follow one another in order, and how Satan has used each of them to weaken the church in this century.

The Second Adam Did Stand Up!

Just as Satan tempted Adam in the beginning, Jesus, the second Adam, had to have his time of testing, too. But how different the conditions were! Adam and Eve had the best of conditions, but Jesus had the worst. Adam and Eve were in a garden; Jesus was in the desert. Adam and Eve were well-fed; Jesus had been fasting forty days and forty nights. In Eden Satan approached the sheep to get to the shepherd. In the wilderness Satan approached the leader directly.

Just as the conditions were different, so was Satan's method. In Eden he came as a benefactor enlightening the poor deluded children to the benefits that were being withheld from them by a selfish God. His goal was to seduce Adam and Eve into sinning. In the wilderness Satan came as an enemy trying to make a treaty. Satan knew if he could bribe Jesus, Jesus' whole mission would be ruined. His goal was to buy Jesus off and divert Him from His purpose using three temptations: pleasure, popularity, and power.

Jesus' three temptations also correspond to three steps downward the church takes as it moves from mildly flirting with Satan to lying seduced in his arms. First, pleasure—the true gospel becomes the "need-meeter gospel." Second, popularity—the church comes to depend more on image than the Holy Spirit. Third, power—our goal becomes dominion over others to be achieved any way we can. Each of the three chapters in this section will examine one of these temptations and how Christ successfully resisted it.

My Kingdom for a Loaf of Bread?

Jesus' first temptation was to use the Holy Spirit's power for His own pleasure. God had set the conditions of the showdown between His Son and Satan. Jesus had been led by the Spirit into the desert to be tempted. It was God's will that Jesus be in the desert for forty days without food and God had not yet given Jesus permission to eat. Satan's first temptation boils down to this: Would Jesus submit to God's timing in providing Him with food, or would He grab for it in His own time on His own terms?

Jesus, as we know, wouldn't sell His kingdom for a loaf of bread. He answered, "Man does not live on bread alone, but on every word that comes from the mouth of God."

"Man Does Not Live by Bread Alone"

Jesus' answer quotes the sermon Moses preached to Israel just before he died. Moses said, "[The Lord] humbled you, causing you to hunger and then feeding you with manna, which neither you nor your fathers had known, to teach you that man does not live on bread alone but on every word that comes from the mouth of the Lord" (Deuteronomy 8:3).

The nation of Israel had experienced the same temptation Jesus experienced—to be stranded in the desert with no food. Israel was supposed to learn that the word of the Lord was more important than anything worldly. God wanted them to learn that they could live without food, without water, without a permanent home, without anything, as long as they had God. Moses had the right attitude when he said, "If your Presence does not go with us, do not send us up from here" (Exodus 33:15).

The generation of Israel that left Egypt didn't learn their lesson. As soon as they got hungry, they grumbled. They remembered the pots of meat they had when they were slaves to the Egyptians. Forgotten were God's promises of a land of milk and honey. Forgotten was God's power demonstrated in the plagues and the crossing of the Red Sea. Though freed from Egypt, Israel was still a nation of slaves, slaves to their stomachs. They would willingly have put themselves under the whip of anyone who would feed them. They did not have the humble faith to "wait in hope for the Lord" (Psalm 33:20). That generation perished in the wilderness.

Forgetting the Glory of God

God didn't mind all that much when they grumbled because they had no food. He provided manna for them. God didn't mind very much when they asked for water. He sweetened the water at Marah and gave them water from a rock at Horeb. But when the Israelites got to the point of criticizing the food God had provided and started talking about appointing a leader to lead them back to Egypt, they had gone too far. They had the glory of the Lord going in front of them in the pillar of cloud during the day and the pillar of fire at night. He had just finished decimating the Egyptians with plagues and leading the whole nation of Israel through the Red Sea, and all they could think about was their stomachs. As the book of Romans says about sinful men in general, although the Israelites "knew God, they neither glorified him as God nor gave thanks to him . . . they exchanged the glory of the immortal God for images . . ." (Romans 1:21-23).

So here we see how this temptation works. The temptation is to *forget the glory of God* by focusing instead on our own needs, desires, or lusts.

Satan: You need a new church building, don't you?

Us: Yes, indeed we do. Meeting in this school building is really inconvenient.

Satan: God has promised to provide all your needs, hasn't He?

Us: Yes, He has.

Satan: Then claim that promise and *order* God to get you a new church building!

What's wrong with Satan's reasoning? Surely God would want a growing church to have its own property, wouldn't He? Maybe He would, and maybe He wouldn't. The problem comes in when we become obsessed with our need to the point of refusing to have any joy in God unless we get what we want in our own way. Instead of saying, "Whether or not God gets us a church building, we will love and glorify Him" we make the *building* the center of our love and excitement. We'll love God, yes, but only if He "blesses" us by stepping down from His Lordship to become our servant.

"Name It and Claim It" . . . or *"Not Thy Will, But Mine"*
Jesus asked God to remove the cup of suffering from Him, but also added, "Nevertheless, not what I want, but what You want." We have to leave the door open for God to say "No"

to our requests, or to provide our needs in different ways from the one we choose. Otherwise, we are letting Satan start to lead us astray.

What happens next looks like this. We have begun to order God to do things our way—not that crassly, of course. We surround our orders with promises of how we will use whatever we get for His glory. We have convinced ourselves that we are showing real faith by setting the dates by which our prayers must be answered or the way in which they must be answered. Then we go on to the next step—inventing *new* needs.

> Satan: You need a wife, don't you?
>
> Us: You bet I do, but I'm beginning to lose hope. I'm homely and don't make enough money. No girl seems interested.
>
> Satan: Then why don't you search Scripture and find a promise you can claim about getting a spouse?

We eagerly pick up our Bibles and start torturing Scripture to find a verse we can twist into a "promise" of this good thing that God, unhappily, never actually promised. Having found it (perhaps the verse in Corinthians about every man having his own wife will do), we then start our temper tantrum, disguised as "praying it through."

"Oh, God, give me a wife! I *need* a wife! I won't have any joy or produce any fruit until I get one! You *promised!*"

When the church hits this phase, she has started to forget how to glorify God. Books start appearing in Christian bookstores that tell you how to pray more effectively, meaning in this case how to find tricks that will force God to give you what you want. Manipulative spiritual techniques start popping up: visualize your desire or thank God in advance for granting it or do this or that good work to earn a goodie from Heaven.

We, meanwhile, are still convinced that we are actually honoring God by this display of selfishness. God is supposedly glorified best when outsiders can see how readily He hops to obey His followers.

Needs to Comforts to Lusts . . . Oh My!

The final stage of this first temptation is when God's people start ordering God to fulfill their sinful lusts. "Oh, Lord, my husband just doesn't fulfill me. I need a better husband." They start pestering the church to act as the means of feeding these lusts. "We need a mixed singles group for divorced couples so we can remarry instead of reconciling with our covenanted wives and husbands." Turn those stones into bread, Lord! Give us what we want right away!

What has been lost here? You are still hearing about "faith" and "God's glory." But there is no spirit of thankfulness or submission. The humble little church praying for its new building has led to prayer meetings where the prayers are for comforts, and that has led to professing believers demanding fulfillment for their lusts. From the Depression family "claiming" new clothes to the fifties family "claiming" a new TV to the eighties singles "claiming" fulfilling careers and scintillating sex lives, the trend has been unmistakably downward.

Happily, unlike pop psychologists who say you need years and years to overcome bad habits, the Bible says Christians can overcome sin in a minute. Just because the church, as a whole, is more enamored at the moment of her own desires than of her Lord, it does not mean we can't change in a moment. And when we do, Satan better watch out!

"Oh, Heavenly Father, Forgive Me . . ."

Edith Schaeffer, in her book *L'Abri,* tells how God led her and her husband Dr. Francis Schaeffer into their world-changing ministry in the Swiss Alps. Through a series of providences, the Schaeffers were forced out of the canton in Switzerland they were using as their home base while they traveled about Europe starting children's Bible clubs. At one point, they had to find a new home in a new district within twenty-four hours or leave Switzerland.

Mrs. Schaeffer tells how she started out all charged up and full of faith that God would find them a new house within the time period. Everyone but her had given up, as the task seemed so impossible. A friend went into premature labor at the last minute and both Schaeffers were commandeered to stay with her all night, leaving only a few hours to find the house. Exhausted, but sturdy in her faith, Mrs. Schaeffer plugged on. The last place on her list turned out to be a lovely, but far too expensive, chalet, and merely discovering the price reduced Mrs. Schaeffer to tears. The owner, a very upper-class woman, thought Mrs. Schaeffer was a bit unsound in the head because of her garbled tale of assisting at a birth all night and needing to find a house in a few minutes, and gently propelled her to the door.

Now let Mrs. Schaeffer say what happened next:

> Feeling I had made an utter fool of myself, I went slowly down her path, and on into deeper snow. There was no place to turn. Suddenly I began to pray.
> "Oh, Heavenly Father, forgive me for my insistence on my own will today. I really do want to want Your will. Please help me to be sincere in this. Forgive me for closing the door in my own attitude toward the possibility of Your having a totally different plan for the next step of our lives. Oh, God, I am willing to live in city slums if it is Your will."

Just a few minutes later, a real estate agent pulled his car up to her and invited her to look over a house with him. That house, Chalet les Melezes, turned out to be the first of the L'Abri homes where hundreds of searching people from around the world would find the answers to their questions and the Lord Jesus Christ.

The Schaeffers' story had what we would consider a happy ending. Some other person's story might have led them into the city slums. When my wife and I prayed that prayer, we found ourselves over the next few years in a succession of mobile homes and inner-city apartments. The point is not that God finally gave Mrs. Schaeffer what she really wanted. The point is that Mrs. Schaeffer finally gave God what He wanted.

Fig Tree Blossom Faith

A long, long time ago a very wise man prayed this prayer:

> Though the fig tree does not bud and there are no grapes on the vines, though the olive crop fails and the fields produce no food, though there are no sheep in the pen and no cattle in the stalls, yet will I rejoice in the LORD, I will be joyful in God my Savior.

What the church needs today is Fig Tree Blossom Faith—the kind of faith that praises God whether we get what we want or whether He tells us to want something else. This kind of faith is invulnerable to the very beginning of the devil's temptations. It rejoices in *God,* not just in His gifts. It says, with the great eighteenth-century evangelist George Whitefield, "Let the name of Jesus be glorified, but the name of Whitefield perish!" It says with the hymnwriter, "Have thine own way, Lord, have thine own way . . . Thou art the potter, I am the clay." This faith rejoices in suffering as well as in comfort, and is as joyful in the Gulag as in the palace of a king. It's the faith of the apostles, of the martyrs, of the missionaries, of the angels!

Jesus had passed the first test. Even while He was almost fainting from hunger, He was more concerned for the glory of God than for His own needs, comforts, or desires. Now He would face a stiffer test, one the modern church at this very moment is in danger of failing. Stay tuned for a look at how the Son of God handled the temptation to clutch for popularity.

7

Flirting with Popularity

Then the devil took him to the holy city and had him stand on the highest point of the temple. "If you are the Son of God," he said, "throw yourself down. For it is written:

" 'He will command his angels concerning you, and they will lift you up in their hands, so that you will not strike your foot against a stone.' "

Jesus answered him, "It is also written: 'Do not put the Lord your God to the test.' "

Matthew 4:5-7

Around our house, it is a proven fact that you *can* reach a man's heart through his stomach. My heart-to-stomach connection is pretty firmly set, especially just before mealtimes!

This must be pretty common among men. A reader of *Focus on the Family* magazine pointed out that, after all the talk about PMS for women, her own husband exhibited all the symptoms: crankiness, inability to cope, pangs in the lower torso—only in his case it was Pre-Meal Syndrome!

But Jesus was different. He would not give up His mission for pleasure—not even for a good meal when He was starving.

The devil, seeing that his fastball had been hit out of the park, decided to throw Jesus a curve. Now he would tempt Jesus to grab for quick popularity. Basically Satan was saying, "If You won't be distracted from Your mission, let me show You a short-cut to Your goal."

"Just Take a Dive"

The devil took Jesus to the highest point of the Temple. People have asked, "Why didn't anyone see Jesus and Satan up there?" The answer is that Satan probably did not physically move Jesus to the pinnacle of the Temple. The Bible says that Jesus "had to be made like his brothers in every way" (Hebrews 2:17) and "we do not have a high priest who is unable to sympathize with our weaknesses, but we have one who has been tempted in every way, just as we are—yet without sin" (Hebrews 4:15). When Satan tempts us, he doesn't physically move us from place to place. He presents pictures to our imagination. If Jesus really was tempted the same way that we are, as the Bible says He was, that means Satan presented a picture to Jesus' mind the same way he does to us. He flashed into Jesus' mind the idea of jumping off the Temple and letting the angels catch Him.

What was the point in Jesus jumping off the pinnacle of the Temple? What would Jesus gain by it?

The Temple was a public place. If Jesus jumped from the high point of the Temple and landed safely, He would be an instant sensation. The Jews were looking for the kind of ruler who could do spectacular miracles. This kind of showboat miracle was what they expected of their Messiah. But Jesus knew why He had come to earth. He knew that His road led through hardship, rejection, and the cross. He knew that any popularity He gained through His teaching, He would quickly lose again. He would gain a large following only after He had died.

Satan was offering Jesus a way to become popular *right away* with a larger proportion of the population—in a way they would not soon forget. Jesus could either go the hard long path God had laid out for Him, or take Satan's way. As we know, Jesus rejected Satan and chose to follow His Father's will.

"OK, If You're God, Now Prove It!"

Satan was tempting Jesus to sin two ways. The first was to show off and draw attention to Himself. Jesus said later, "The greatest among you will be your servant. For whoever exalts himself will be humbled, and whoever humbles himself will be exalted." God does not like show-offs.

The second sin was testing God—demanding that God prove He is God by performing a miracle on request. Jesus' answer to this temptation quotes Moses again from Deuteronomy 6:16: "Do not test the Lord your God as you did at Massah."

Massah, which means *testing*, is the name Moses gave to Rephidim, a place along Israel's journey. The Israelites quarreled with Moses there because there was no water. Exodus 17:7 says, "And he called the place Massah and Meribah [quarreling] because the Israelites quarreled and because they tested the Lord saying, 'Is the Lord among us or not?'"

Did the Israelites need more proof that God was with them? They had experienced the plagues. They had crossed the Red Sea on dry ground. They had received the manna and the quail in the desert. The pillar of cloud went in front of them during the day, and the pillar of fire by night. If they needed more proof, then there's a market for snowballs in Alaska!

The Israelites had fallen prey to Satan's temptation to order God around by claiming a promise. They were thirsty. They wanted water yesterday, if not sooner. God had promised to be their God; therefore, He had to provide them water. If He didn't come through, they would not let Him stay their God. They would search for another one who kept them better supplied. What a mistake!

The people of Israel were looking at their relationship to God entirely backwards. They should have remembered that *they* hadn't chosen *God*, after all—*God* had chosen *them*. God wasn't obligated to supply them with water the instant they threw a tantrum. They, however, were obligated to obey and trust God. God had promised to be their God and provide for them, yet He was still God and reserved the right to provide in His own time. Their job was to meekly pray for what they needed and submissively wait for God's answer.

That generation of Israel never learned the lesson. They died in the wilderness.

Jesus knew that God was with Him. Hadn't God just proclaimed, "This is my Son, whom I love; with him I am well pleased"? Jesus didn't need any grandiose miracle to prove He was the Son of God! To test God would have been sinful.

Bless For Success

People today are still using the Temple as their jumping-off point for personal success. See if the following scenario rings a bell: A man, maybe a television preacher or leader of a large Christian ministry, gets an idea for a grandiose project for him to head up. Maybe it's a new university, or maybe he decides to evangelize all Africa. He then figures out how much money he will need to finish his project.

At this point, the godly thing to do is what Christian Liberty Academy did when they got the opportunity to buy a public school campus in Arlington Heights, Illinois. They brought the project to God and the Christian home-schooling public. The immediate enthusiastic support and pledges of more money later encouraged them to go ahead and they now own that public school.

But our Christian entrepreneur claims that this is walking by sight. He goes out on a limb. He borrows the money and *then* goes public with his plan:

"God has given me the vision for a great new project, brothers and sisters. We have been led to buy a facility just outside of Pioneer, Georgia for our new world headquarters.

"But we need your help, brothers and sisters, to make this great vision a reality. If we don't receive donations totalling $100,000 by the end of this month, this whole grand dream will end and all of God's money that we have poured into the project so far will be lost. . . ."

Men have preached that if you go out on a limb and cut it off, that provides a great opportunity for God to be glorified. When God bails you out of your impossible predicament, you can praise Him for his wonderful power and provision. You get what you were after. God gets praise. Everyone is happy! Right?

What if God sovereignly decides that the church of Jesus Christ doesn't need a new university or that this man is not the one to convert all Africa? The bank forecloses on the loan, giving Christians in general a bad credit rating. The equity on the property is wasted. And most importantly, since the preacher used God's name when he was pushing the project, non-Christians can point to this failure as a sign that God either isn't there, or couldn't pull it off.

But God surely wouldn't let something like this happen, would He? He is jealous for His name, isn't He?

God might cause a project like this to fail, just because He *is* jealous for His name. Will the God of the universe let every Tom, Dick, and Harry who uses God's name in a sales pitch manipulate Him? Then there really would be a stain on His name! Non-Christians are more likely to call the man who tried the grandstand play a fool than to question God. Avoiding just this embarrassing possibility of being called a fool leads to the sin of trying to create and maintain an image.

Polishing the Image

The Commander in the film *The Gospel Blimp* is an excellent example of what I'm talking about. The Commander wasn't in town when the blimp P.A. system fouled up and imposed the sound of a Polish gospel broadcast onto everyone's favorite TV show. When he returned the next day, the Commander axed the pilot, who wasn't at fault, and issued a press release blaming everyone beside himself for the debacle. The release claimed that if the Commander had been there, this never would have happened.

The new public relations man explained to the Gospel Blimp board that he was glad that the Commander had been out of town. They all knew that he couldn't have done anything to avert the disaster, but the public must continue to believe in him. The Commander's image must be preserved at all costs!

The P.R. man said people can't identify with an idea, or even with the blimp. They needed a man to represent the blimp. That man was the Commander. Therefore the Commander's image must be maintained spotless. So the Commander wrecked the career of a young pilot and lied to the public.

Image or Reality?

Image. That's the word! Dress for success. Have your hair styled. Keep those nails in good shape. Be sure to polish the backs of your shoes. You have to keep up that image if you're going to succeed in this world!

The church has to exist in this world, too, doesn't it? Therefore the church and its representatives have to maintain their image, or God will look like a shabby God, right? But what is an image? "Image" can mean a picture or exact copy of something. But "image" can also mean counterfeit, delusion, fantasy, illusion, or figment. This second meaning is a lot closer to the modern use of the word. If a presidential candidate can change his image from appealing to the farmers of Iowa to appealing to the high-flying businessmen of New York in the space of two weeks and just by changing his clothes, then how much can the image reflect the true man?

Our God wants us to worship Him in spirit and in truth. Hebrews 10:22 says, ". . . let us draw near to God with a sincere heart in full assurance of faith . . ." Creating an image for ourselves is the opposite of truth and sincerity. God looks shabby only when it appears to the world that He countenances a bunch of hypocrites for worshippers.

Dress to Impress

When we lived in the South, some Christians there impressed on us the need to dress well so that we would be a "witness." A gorgeous and expensive outward appearance is a witness, all right. But a witness to what? You can't even tell a well-dressed Christian from a tastefully-dressed non-Christian just by looking at her. What you *can* often see is an hour a day spent primping, an hour a day spent on the Jane Fonda workout, and another hour spent on shopping or on keeping up with the fashion magazines. And, in the end, all this does not lead to the world marching to our door to be converted, since the

Mormons are often better-looking than we are and Christian Scientists are richer.

Close cousin to the quest for beauty is the stress on fitness. One denominational magazine printed an article a couple of years back in which the author said we should spend as much time in exercise as we do in prayer and Bible study. A church in that same denomination refused to call a minister because his wife, who had just had a baby, was too plump for their liking. They thought she wouldn't give the church a good image.

If outward appearance led people to Christ, what in the world was God doing sending John the Baptist, a man who ate grasshoppers and dressed in a simple garment of camel's hair, as the prophet to announce the arrival of Jesus?

Face it—the road to Heaven is not paved with melba toast and aerobic workouts. Nor is it paved with BMW's, Reebok shoes, and designer haircuts.

"Thou Shalt Not Make Unto Thee Any . . . Image"

The Bible puts little stress on image, except to insist that we not worship it. When God sent Samuel to Jesse's house in Bethlehem to anoint the new king to replace Saul, Samuel was impressed by Jesse's oldest son:

> When they arrived, Samuel saw Eliab and thought, "Surely the Lord's anointed stands before the Lord."
>
> But the Lord said to Samuel, "Do not consider his appearance or his height, for I have rejected him. The Lord does not look at the things man looks at. Man looks at the outward appearance, but the Lord looks at the heart."

Peter writes,

> Your beauty should not come first from outward adornment, such as braided hair and the wearing of gold jewelry and fine clothes. Instead it should be that of your inner self, the unfading beauty of a gentle and quiet spirit, which is of great worth in God's sight. For this is the way the holy women of the past who put their hope in God used to make themselves beautiful, like Sarah, who obeyed Abraham and called him her master. (1 Peter 3:3-6)

Proverbs says, "Like a gold ring in a pig's snout is a beautiful woman who shows no discretion" (Proverbs 11:22). God doesn't look at our outside appearance. What matters most to God is a pure heart.

Jesus talks about John the Baptist's image:

> Jesus began to speak to the crowd about John: "What did you go out into the desert to see? A reed swayed by the wind? If not, what did you go out to see? A man dressed in fine clothes? No, those who wear fine clothes are in kings' palaces. Then what did you go out to see? A prophet? Yes, I tell you, and more than a prophet."

John was not a fashion plate. Yet the people of Israel went out to see him, to hear him, and to repent and be baptized by him. The important thing was not what John looked like, but who he was.

Isaiah says of the Christ, "He has no beauty or majesty to attract us to him, nothing in his appearance that we should desire him." Jesus Christ Himself had no image.

Performance Worship

More and more, the worship of God has become a matter of image. The building has to be impressive, preferably with a pipe organ. The choir has to be decked out in robes and sing flawlessly. Children must not be allowed in the service, because their fussing or taking trips to the bathroom in the middle of the sermon will destroy the worshipful atmosphere. The preaching should be eloquent, entertaining, and in good taste—no preaching about Hell, the wrath of God, and so on so you don't offend visitors. The important thing is that Sunday morning be a well-executed work of art to present to God.

The following two stories (both possibly apocryphal) illustrate the contrast I am trying to draw.

Three Scottish preachers visiting London decided to visit the churches of two of London's foremost preachers and compare the two. After they left the first church service, one of them exclaimed, "What a great sermon that man preached!"

They then proceeded to the second church, pastored by C. H. Spurgeon. This time they left in tears rejoicing, "What a great God we have!" The first man impressed his guests with his knowledge of Scripture and his eloquence. Spurgeon impressed them with God.

A similar story concerns a church service in which a professional actor was asked to read Psalm 23. With marvelous intonation and expression the actor read the Psalm. When he was done, all the audience burst into spontaneous applause. Suddenly an old man stood up. "That's not right!" he husked. "Let me read that psalm the way it ought to be read." Limping to the podium, he faced the congregation and began to recite the Psalm by heart, beginning with, "The Lord is *my* shepherd. . ." He wasn't polished and his diction wasn't perfect, but when he was done, the audience was in tears. Someone asked the actor afterward why he thought the old man had produced so profound an effect on his hearers. The actor said, "I only knew the Psalm. That man knows the shepherd."

Are You Washed in the Blood of the Lamb?

Now it's time for the $64,000 question: *Why* has the church become so enthralled with image? Here's the answer: We are substituting image for God. We are in danger of trying to lead people, not to God, but to ourselves. We want them to be impressed by *us,* to rally around *us,* to say, "What marvelous people you must be if you can jump off a Temple and walk away from it!"

The single most serious symptom of this substitution of images for God, and the easiest to correct, is what has happened to the gospel message. We have become salesmen instead of prophets, toning down our "product's" negative angles and putting all our stress on what we think will sell. We are leaving out the cross. We are leaving out the blood of Jesus.

The Bible says that the cross is a stumbling-block to the world. That's absolutely true, and there's no legitimate way around it. We have no business preaching forgiveness and love and Heaven and personal change without also preaching repentance and death to the old man. Sure, our intentions are good. We want to make it easier for people to come to Christ. But we are doing them no favors when we tell them to come in an impossible way—to come to life without having first been slain, to come to God without first being washed in the blood of the Lamb.

A. W. Tozer puts it feelingly:

> We who preach the gospel must not think of ourselves as public relations agents sent to establish good will between Christ and the world. We must not imagine ourselves commissioned to make Christ acceptable to big business, the press, the world of sports or modern education. We are not diplomats but prophets, and our message is not a compromise but an ultimatum.

It's so, so much easier to sell ourselves, to make friends and influence people, than it is to tell sinners they must die and be born again. It's so much easier try to impress the messengers of the king of Babylon with our riches than it is to tell them that our God is the one true God and they are worshiping idols.

The Bible tells us nothing of a "personal Savior" that we have to "accept." You may have a "personal computer" or a "personal secretary," but Christ is no hip-pocket Savior. Nor is eternal life a casual gift that God is begging us to accept without cost or pain. It costs everything we have: our lives, our fortunes, and our sacred honor. As Jesus said, we have to count the cost before even beginning to follow Him, because there *is* a cost.

It's the Real Thing!

It's time to give up the cross-free gospel. Not only is it fraud and false advertising (we tell people *after* they get "saved" that now they have to turn around their lives!), but it doesn't even work.

Just as Pharaoh was unimpressed by the miracles of Moses as long as his magicians could duplicate the miracles, the world is not moved by outward image. They, too, can have pipe organs, choirs, beautiful entertainers, scintillating speakers, and so on. These things are not *wrong,* they just are not an adequate substitute for the power of God.

The Bible tells us what kind of "image" will impress the world. Jesus said, "A new command I give you: Love one another. As I have loved you, so you must love one another. By this all men will know that you are my disciples, if you love one another."

The world is not impressed by our amateurish attempts to impress it. But when we have the real thing, the world will know it!

As we have seen, the church has fallen at least partially prey to the temptation to pursue our own pleasure rather than the glory of God, and to the temptation to chase after worldly popularity. Now that we evangelicals have made it to that pinnacle of popularity, the cover of *Time* magazine, we are suddenly faced with a brand-new temptation—the urge to personal power. We'll see how Satan is right now dangling that bait before us, and how Jesus has taught us to handle that temptation, in the next chapter.

8

Flirting with Power

Again the devil took him to a very high mountain and showed him all the kingdoms of the world and their splendor. "All this will I give you," he said, "if you will bow down and worship me."

Jesus said to him, "Away from me, Satan! For it is written: 'Worship the Lord your God, and serve him only.'"

Then the devil left him, and angels came and attended him.

Matthew 4:8-11

As a family, we Prides like to improve our minds by watching highbrow videos. One such video, *The Mark of Zorro,* is a favorite at our house, ranking right up there with the version of *The Adventures of Robin Hood* starring Errol Flynn.

These videos may not be all that intellectual, but they *are* educational, sparking all kinds of discussion about the proper response to tyranny, how to behave like a chivalrous gentleman, and so forth. One scene in *The Mark of Zorro,* for example, illustrates the difference between totalitarian rule and servant rule. Martinez, a convicted murderer, is being bribed by the Spanish Commandante of Los Angeles into posing as Zorro, a heroic outlaw. The Commandante complains to Martinez that he can't catch Zorro because the people hide Zorro from his soldiers, thinking Zorro is their friend.

"Whereas it is *you* who are their friend," Martinez replies ironically.

"Exactly!" says the Commandante.

He then gives Martinez his instructions. Dressed as Zorro, Martinez is to rob and humiliate everyone attending a party given by the Commandante, especially the servants and the poor people.

"And what if one of them resists?" Martinez inquires.

The Commandante, exasperated by Martinez's seeming slowness to comprehend, tells him that, of course, he should fight anyone who resists him, killing them if necessary.

Martinez closes the scene by saying with not-too-well-veiled sarcasm, "I bow to a true friend of the people."

Satan's Side of the Mountain

Jesus' third temptation, the temptation to seize earthly power, was a mountaintop experience. Again, we know that this is not a literal mountain. No mountain in the world is high enough to see all the nations of the earth from its top. Mountains are used to describe a seat of political power. Think of Mount Seir which stands for Edom, or Mount Samaria which stands for Israel, or Mount Zion which stands for either Jerusalem and Judah or God's throne in Heaven.

In Daniel 2, Nebuchadnezzar's dream ended when a small stone cut out of the mountain without hands grew to be a mountain which filled the whole earth. Daniel interpreted this little stone as "a kingdom which will never be destroyed" (Daniel 2:44). Satan's exceedingly high mountain was probably his seat of power from which he ruled over the kingdoms of men. From there Jesus could spiritually see all the kingdoms of the earth and all their splendor.

For Jesus to desire lordship over the earth was not wrong. The Father, the *King* (Psalm 10:16), had promised Him the kingdoms of the earth as His inheritance (Psalm 2:7-9). It would have been wrong for Jesus to grab power Satan's way. Satan was again tempting Jesus with a shortcut. Satan would make Jesus ruler of all the kingdoms of the earth if Jesus would just worship him. Jesus would not have to suffer rejection. Jesus would not have to submit to the cross. He could have it all right now without the grief He would have to suffer if He took God's route. He could be like God, ruling the kingdoms of the earth.

The Kings of the Gentiles

Jesus had to choose between two kinds of lordship: to rule as the kings of the Gentiles rule or to rule God's way. Satan was trying to tempt Him to grasp the first kind of power—to become the Big Boss. This is the only way Satan knows how to rule: raw totalitarian power.

Jesus describes totalitarian power this way: "The kings of the Gentiles lord it over them; and those who exercise authority over them call themselves Benefactors" (Luke 22:25). Think of Hitler, Lenin, and Stalin. Did they think they were the enemies of their countries? Of course not. Each one thought he was the best thing that had ever happened to his country. They were the great servants of the people—benefactors. And in order to preserve the "blessing" of their rules, Hitler had his Gestapo, and Lenin and Stalin had their secret police.

When the Mafia moves into a neighborhood it doesn't come to the common people wielding guns. They come as benefactors who will keep the other gangs from bothering the innocent folks and who will control the petty criminals. When they get into city government, they make sure the roads in their territory are well paved and the parks well kept. But they extort a high price both in money and fear for their "protection."

The Trainer and the Shepherd

The kings of the Gentiles lord it over them. But Jesus says,

> You are not to be like that. Instead, the greatest among you should be like the youngest, and the one who rules like the one who serves. For who is greater, the one who is at the table or the one who serves? Is it not the one who is at the table? But I am among you as one who serves. (Luke 22:26, 27)

Jesus said that a Christian ruler must be like one who serves. He uses Himself as an example, saying, "Whoever wants to become great among you must be your servant, and whoever wants to be first must be slave of all. For even the Son of Man did not come to be served, but to serve, and to give his life as a ransom for many" (Mark 10:43-45).

Leaders in the church are not dictators, but servant-leaders. Authority leads to responsibility, not to power. The larger your flock the greater your area of service.

A leader under Christ is like a boxer's trainer. The boxer—even if he hires the trainer himself—submits himself to the care of the trainer. The trainer tells the boxer what to eat, how much exercise and what kind of exercises to do, and how much sleep to get. The trainer may set a curfew and enforce it. The trainer's job is to develop the boxer into a better boxer so that he can win. The trainer and boxer both benefit if the boxer succeeds.

A Christian leader's job is to strengthen the people under his care. He serves them for their good. An elder has to be able to teach—the spiritual equivalent to feeding his flock. He should be able to recommend a spiritual diet to his flock by being well versed in Scripture and well read in Christian literature. His goal is to make sure that his flock grows and thrives.

Another, more Scriptural, analogy is a shepherd. A good shepherd will prepare good pastures for his flock and find good watering places. He will inspect his sheep for disease and treat them if they are sick. He will wash them and free them from insect pests. If any of them stray, he searches for them. He makes sure none of the sheep bully the weaker ones.

A leader in the church should have the same relationship with his "sheep." "Anyone who receives instruction in the word must share all good things with his instructor" (Galatians 6:6). The instructor in return feeds (teaches) his students and protects them from enemies both outside and inside the church.

Hoard of the Rings

Satan comes to us with the same temptation to power. He says, "If you will just worship me and follow my methods you will have power, then you can do what you want with it. Power is power to do good also, you know."

The main theme of Tolkien's *Lord of the Rings* trilogy was the destruction of the one Ring of Power. One of the elves had forged rings which had various powers associated with them. Three were given to elf lords, seven to the dwarves, and nine were wielded by men. Sauron, the evil lord, knew of the rings and had forged one Ring to rule all the other rings. When he was overthrown, the Ring, which should have been destroyed, was lost instead. Centuries later the Ring was found again by a hobbit, Bilbo Baggins. The trilogy begins with Bilbo passing the Ring on to his heir, Frodo Baggins.

Gandalf, the good wizard, discovered the lore of the rings and urged Frodo to leave his home in the Shire and take the Ring to some safer abode. Frodo, in terror, tried to give the Ring to Gandalf.

> "But I have so little use of any of these things! You are wise and powerful. Will you take the Ring?"
>
> "No!" cried Gandalf . . . "Do not tempt me! For I do not wish to become like the Dark Lord himself. Yet the way of the Ring to my heart is pity, pity for the weakness and the desire of strength to do good. Do not tempt me! I dare not take it, not even to keep it safe, unused."

Gandalf was tempted to take the Ring in order to do good with it, but he knew that in wielding the enemy's tools he would become just like the enemy.

We face the same danger if we use Satan's methods to do our work. Satan's servants work through intrigues, power plays, confederations, bribes, threats, bluff, propaganda, and compromise. These methods are inappropriate for a Christian.

The Jewish leaders during Jesus' time were adept at this kind of politicking from dealing with the Romans. When they saw Jesus gathering such large popular support they were afraid. They feared the crowds. They knew what they would do with if they had a following like that and expected Jesus to do the same. Both they and the people were confused and shocked when He didn't. Jesus was working by different rules than the ones they were used to.

"Take Up Your Cross" or Hitch a Ride on the Beast?

We know how Jesus answered this temptation. Jesus quoted Moses again, "Worship the Lord your God, and serve him only" (Deuteronomy 6:13). Jesus' point of view is described in Philippians 2:

> Your attitude should be the same as that of Christ Jesus:
> Who being in very nature God, did not consider equality with God something to be grasped, but made himself nothing, taking the very nature of a servant, being made in human likeness.
> And being found in appearance as a man, he humbled himself and became obedient to death—even death on a cross!

Unlike Adam, who did consider being like God something to grasp, Jesus humbled Himself and became a servant. He denied Himself, something very few of us are taught consistently to do these days. Although Jesus was God, as a man He gave us the example of service to God as the antidote for the temptation to power.

The church today faces perilous times, just as the hobbits and other good folk in *The Lord of the Rings* faced perilous times. We see the incredible corruption in our society and begin to think we should do something about it. That is correct. The church is supposed to be salt, which keeps society pure, and leaven, which spreads God's message through the land. But *how* are we supposed to accomplish these goals? By setting our sights first on obtaining power, so we can "do good" with it, or by doing good right here and now and trusting the Lord to bless our efforts with further authority?

The book of Revelation shows a picture of what the church becomes when she strives to take authority over the rest of society without putting God first. By degrees, this church finds herself compromising, then giving away her position wholesale and even persecuting true believers, as she enters wholeheartedly into the quest for power. She ends up as a harlot whose temporary ride on the Beast (symbolizing the evil power structures in this world) comes to a quick and bloody end when the Beast turns on her, eats her flesh, and burns her with fire (Revelation 17).

Shine the Light and Pass the Salt

All questions of eschatology aside, the fact remains that the church *is* supposed to have an influence in this world and that we are *not* supposed to run after personal power, titles, and glory. The harlot's prayer is, "Hallowed be *my* name. *My* kingdom come, *my* will be done on heaven as it is on earth." The Christian view of dominion is spiritual: "Our Father who art in heaven, hallowed be *Thy* name. *Thy* kingdom come, *Thy* will be done on earth as it is in heaven."

Once we, like Jesus, have laid aside all personal earthly ambition and the desire to take the easy road, the path to heavenly power opens up. We have the *light,* which is the truth of God's Word. This is a powerful double-edged sword that indeed "subdues nations under us" (Psalm 47). We have the *salt,* which is our service to others. He who is the servant of all does become the greatest in God's kingdom. He has the spiritual power and authority to influence worldly powers and authorities. Look at the history of Christian missions, from the first century on, to see what an effect the light and the salt combined have on the history of nations.

As long as we Christians don't care who among men gets the glory as long as God's name is honored and His kingdom advanced, God's name *will* be honored and His kingdom advanced. We don't need to surrender our doctrine or our standards or make alliances with the heathen to have kingdom power. As individual citizens of this world we may find ourselves at times working with non-Christians for political goals—but we never need to go begging the world *as Christians.* The church can build up the Lord's house alone, and does not need the help of the Samaritans (Ezra 4:1-3). Nor do we come to our political leaders with sticks and bludgeons, throwing around our weight and boasting of our numbers. The *meek,* not the nasty, shall inherit the earth.

"Therefore, You Kings, Be Wise"

Jesus told people how to behave, but He told them first how to think, and first of all how to be born again. Any revival of church interest in government that is not thoroughly salted with the preaching of the blood of Jesus as the one way to salvation is doomed to the fate of the harlot of Revelation 17. We are told to tone down our religion and not scare our leaders with our blood-and-thunder message. This, however, is exactly the message they need to hear, both as individual men and women and as responsible leaders of a nation. God gives priority to this message, placing it second in the Book of Psalms only to the need for choosing salvation.

> Therefore, you kings, be wise;
>   be warned, you rulers of the earth.
> Serve the Lord with fear
>   and rejoice with trembling.
> Kiss [that is, embrace] the Son, lest he be angry
>   and you be destroyed in your way. . . . (Psalm 2:10-12)

How is the church to regain the courage and power to preach this way to individual sinners, let alone to the heads of nations? The answer lies in Genesis 3.

In the first part of this book we saw how Satan successfully tempted Adam and Eve, causing the downfall of the entire human race. Now we will turn those temptations around and go back through them in reverse order. For each bite of the snake, we will see what antidote God's Word prescribes. When we finish looking at these temptations, we will see just exactly what steps the church today needs to take to shake herself free of Satan and once again stand as a beacon to the nations.

PART THREE

In the World

> "You are the light of the world. A city on a hill cannot be hidden. Neither do people light a lamp and put it under a bowl. Instead they put it on its stand, and it gives light to everyone in the house. In the same way, let your light shine before men, that they may see your good deeds and praise your Father in heaven."
>
> Matthew 5:14-16

9

Walk Like a Man

> *O thus be it ever when free men shall stand
> Between their loved homes and the war's desolation . . .*
> — Francis Scott Key, "The Star-Spangled Banner"

> *The reason I [Paul] left you [Titus] in Crete was that you might straighten out what was left unfinished and appoint elders in every town, as I directed you. An elder must be blameless, the husband of but one wife, a man whose children believe and are not open to the charge of being wild and disobedient. . . . He must hold firmly to the trustworthy message as it has been taught, so that he can encourage others by sound doctrine and refute those who oppose it.*
> *For there are many rebellious people, mere talkers and deceivers . . . They must be silenced . . .*
> — Titus 1:5-8

THE SCENE: Main Street. A lonely sagebrush rolls through the dust as two burly gunmen stalk towards each other down the middle of the street, hands poised over the handles of their six-shooters.

THE CHARACTERS: some nameless character actor as mean, worthless, widow-making sidewinder Black Bart, Ms. Gloria Liberated as the Schoolmarm, and John Wayne as (who else?) the Sheriff.

THE ACTION: As Wayne and Black Bart square off for their shootout, the schoolmarm dashes from the sidewalk. Plucking at John Wayne's sleeve, she pleads with him in nasal tones to throw away his gun. "It's not fair!" she wails. "Gunfighting shouldn't be legal!"

"Fair or not," John Wayne informs her, "seein' as Black Bart here is gonna try 'n shoot me in about three seconds, I figger as I better shoot back."

Switching tactics, the schoolteacher continues to plead. "Don't shoot him! He'll go away if you ignore him."

"Ma'am," Wayne replies, "if I ignore him he'll shoot me dead."

Undeterred, the schoolteacher brushes back her bun and fixes Wayne with a cold eye. "Lots of us like the way Black Bart has been running this town and we don't *want* you to shoot him. Give me that gun!"

What would John Wayne do then? Droop his shoulders and meekly hand over his gun, muttering under his breath, "I guess Black Bart's killing twenty people and stealing all the bank's money wasn't *really* that bad"? Or would he resolutely square his chin, tug his hat down, stare right back at the schoolteacher and grate out, "Sorry, Ma'am, *I'm* the sheriff and I'm a-gonna silence this murdering desperado whether it pleases you and your pals or not!"

Don't Give Up the Ship!

In real life, or Hollywood life, for that matter, you can't imagine John Wayne letting some nagging lobbyist shame him into denying his pledged word and giving up on a job. That's because John Wayne was the very symbol of a Real Man—someone who knew how to live up to his authority.

In Chapter Five we saw how Adam failed to live up to his authority by letting Eve take the lead in talking to Satan. Adam let Eve lead so that if anything went wrong, he could blame her for the decision. God wasn't fooled. God held Adam responsible for the decision he had let Eve make for the two of them.

When God gives you a position of authority, He will hold you responsible for everything that goes on under your command. A father is responsible for his household. A magistrate is responsible for the municipality he presides over. And a church leader—pastor, elder, deacon—or an older woman who instructs younger women is responsible for the flock God assigns him or her. God wants a leader to take responsibility for his command.

"You Just Can't Expect People . . ."

When there is an uprising in the ranks it used to be that the head tried to control the insubordination of those under him. Now he makes excuses for them.

Imagine a general inspecting a base. He looks in the kitchen and finds all the pots and kitchen tools lying in and around the sink all filthy. The cook is sprawled in a chair smoking a cigar and playing cribbage with the dishwasher.

The general sticks his head in the barracks door, but recoils back from the smell. Uniforms lie on the floor or are draped over the ends of the unmade beds. The officer's mess lives up to its name, and their quarters aren't much better than the barracks.

When he confronts the commanding officer with the state of his command, all the C.O. has for an answer is, "You just can't expect soldiers to clean up after themselves in this day and age." Would the general accept that answer? No, of course not! He would dress down that soon-to-be-ex-C.O. in the saltiest language in his vocabulary. The main theme of the sermon would be, "It's *your* job to make *sure* they do it!"

Adam could have stopped Eve from eating the fruit if he had wanted to. He could have broken in on her conversation with the serpent. He could have physically restrained her from eating the fruit if he let things go so far. But Adam let things take their course, listened to his wife, and ate from the tree (Genesis 3:17). God held him responsible.

Jesus, our general, won't accept "You just can't expect . . ." from us, either. "You just can't expect kids to respect their elders." "You just can't expect church folk to tithe anymore." "You can't expect teenagers to listen to sermons about sin and God's wrath." "You can't expect men to give up watching football on Sunday!" True, a church is not the army. In the church you can't *make* anyone do things (although let's not underestimate the power of preacher pressure), but you can *tell* them what to do, *make it possible* for them to do what's right, and *silence* those who refuse to obey God's plain word.

Paul wrote Titus:

> For there are many rebellious people, mere talkers and deceivers, especially those of the circumcision group. They must be silenced, because they are ruining whole households by teaching things they ought not to teach. (Titus 1:10, 11)

If we can't expect those under godly authority to behave nowadays, it's only because there are so many unsilenced false teachers running around. Left to himself, Joe Christian doesn't decide to reinvent the Bible or break away from traditional Christian morality. An occasional sheep might stray, but it takes a wolf in shepherd's clothing to lead the whole flock over a cliff!

Very little modern Christian literature deals with the problem of confronting false teachers *within* the church. Perhaps that's why we have so many now! We don't know how to recognize them, or what to do about them.

So far in this book we've looked at the different false *teachings* Satan tries to inflict on us. Now let's see what we're supposed to do about false *teachers!*

The Great American Know-Nothings

Paul says false teachers "must be silenced." Who are these people who ought to be silenced? Paul calls them "mere talkers and deceivers" and says they are teaching things that they ought not to teach. "These are the kind," Paul wrote to Timothy, "who worm their way into homes." What do they do when they get into your home? They "gain control over weak-willed women . . . always learning but never able to acknowledge the truth" (2 Timothy 3:6, 7).

We have got to start realizing that evil teaching doesn't come all dressed up in drag and carrying a sign announcing, "I

Am An Evil Teaching." Those who would push us into the fire start by filling the room with smoke. They don't say, for example, "We want you to throw out everything the Bible teaches about homosexuality being an evil sin and accept it as a good and normal way to live." Instead, they say, "What makes you think you know so much about what kind of sexuality is right and wrong? Does the Bible *really* condemn all forms of sexual expression outside of heterosexual marriage? Aren't there lots of ways of interpreting those texts you are so fond of quoting?" And so on.

This is the spirit of *relativism*. Kids are taught relativism in the public schools, from kindergarten on. It's preached on television and in magazines. Nowadays in America the one cardinal sin is to say that something is right or wrong. As bestselling author Allan Bloom says in his *Closing of the American Mind,* "There is one thing a professor can be absolutely certain of: almost every student entering the university believes, or says he believes, that truth is relative."

These are the Know-Nothings who Paul was talking about. They know everything except that right is right and wrong is wrong. By "ever learning"—that is, continually studying and reopening issues that ought to be closed—they manage never to acknowledge the truth.

Pilate Said "What Is Truth?" Just Before He Crucified Christ

Know-Nothingism has infested the church. How many times have you gotten into a discussion with other Christians and had someone shut you down with something like: "That may be O.K. for *you,* but I just can't buy it"; or "*My* God wouldn't make people do that (or prevent people from doing that)"? How many times have you heard:

- "There is no easy answer" (on questions of right and wrong).
- "The Bible is silent on this issue."

- "That may have been right back then, but times have changed."
- "It's not just simple black and white. There are shades of gray."

The speaker, having asserted that there is no Biblical position on the issue he is discussing, goes on to hustle his particular agenda.

But, of course, as Jesus could have told Pilate had the latter waited around long enough to hear, there *is* such a thing as truth and we can know it. Jesus Christ is "the Way and the Truth and the Life," not "the Groping and the Wondering and the Doubt." There *are* easy answers: Thou Shalt Not Steal and Thou Shalt Not Commit Adultery. The Bible is never silent—muzzled, maybe, but not silent. Times have not changed God or His Law, and people who revel in those supposed shades of gray just turn out to be rolling in plain old dirt.

Even Allan Bloom, who is in no way a Christian, knows "there are two kinds of openness" and that along with "the openness that invites us to the quest for knowledge and certitude" there is a phony openness "promoted with the twin purposes of humbling our intellectual pride and letting us be whatever we want to be, just as long as we don't want to be knowers."

"They Must Be Silenced, For They Are Ruining Whole Households"

The men in Crete whom Titus was supposed to silence were "ruining whole households by teaching things they ought not to teach" (Titus 1:11).

How do false teachers ruin households today? Households, including the church, run on ministry. A mother caring for her children, a husband taking out the trash for his wife, a son doing the dishes for his mother, are all examples of ministry. But Know-Nothings *attack* ministry!

One of the favorite tactics of the Know-Nothings is to claim they are trying to save people from guilt feelings. They don't want those who are not ministering to feel guilty, so they downplay the value of every kind of unpaid ministry, especially ministry in the family. But if denying yourself and serving others is no more valuable than indulging yourself and palming off your own work on others, why should anyone make the effort to serve? Thus, although the Know-Nothings initially appear to only want "equal time" for "alternative lifestyles," they actually end up ripping the guts out of the traditional (read, Biblical) family.

You want an example of what I'm talking about? Try reading any baby, women's, or parents' magazine on the market. I could cite a thousand examples, but for the moment let's just take what they have to say about breastfeeding. The articles invariably begin by praising the virtues of breastfeeding and saying that breastfeeding is the best thing for your baby. They just as invariably go on to tell you that bottle-feeding is just as good, winding up with some sentence like, "Regardless of whether you choose to breastfeed or bottle-feed, you can be sure that you are doing the best for yourself and your baby." After reading an article like that, what incentive does a mother have to make herself available to her baby at all hours of the day and night, when her husband or a baby-sitter and a bottle can do just as well?

Dr. James Dobson had the courage in a booklet quoted in his *Focus on the Family* magazine to suggest that a mom-at-home is performing a useful function. He said:

> The decision for Mom to work has profound implications for her family, and especially for her children. That decision must be made in the full light of reality, being unedited by the biases of the women's movement. And most importantly, we dare not strip the dignity from the most noble occupation in the universe—that of molding little lives during their period of greatest vulnerability.

He qualified his view thoroughly with statements like, "The decision to have a career or to be a homemaker is an intensely personal choice," and because some women have to work, "Christian onlookers should should express tolerant understanding . . ."

Quite predictably, he got a complaining letter from a mother who worked outside of her home. She ended like this:

> It is my belief that there is room in God's will for the working mother, and that she needs emotional and spiritual support.
>
> I would like to see some articles directed to the working mother in your magazine.

Let's look at what that woman was *really* saying. She couldn't have meant that she can't get emotional and spiritual support anywhere unless Dr. Dobson provides it, because 99% of secular magazines and 98% of Christian magazines *already* promote, encourage, and support women who put their children in day-care. That being so, we see her *real* demand: "Dr. Dobson, please stop encouraging stay-at-home moms. I demand that you announce that availing yourself of two incomes and handing one's children voluntarily over to strangers is *just as good* as raising them yourself." She couldn't bear to see mothers who make the sacrifice of working at home getting any special honor.

The Carrot and the Stick

The pathetic condition of the home, the church, and the nation today is simply what you get when you let loud, angry, non-ministering people go on demanding that they receive equal honor with those who sacrifice to do God's work. If you refuse them this honor, they claim you are setting yourself up as "better" than them—a scurrilous sin indeed!

Apparently we are not supposed to make anyone feel bad, ever. That would flood him with guilt feelings that crush his fragile self-esteem and keep him from ever getting better. The flip side of this doctrine, as we have seen, is that we are supposed to make everyone feel good.

This destroys all basis for authority. It removes both the carrot (giving special honor to those who deserve it) and the stick (shaming or chastising those who do wrong.) But God knows leaders can't exercise authority armed only with carrots!

That is why He gave leaders in every sphere both a carrot and a stick.

- State leaders have the "sword" (Romans 13:4) to "punish those who do wrong," and also the authority to "commend those who do right" (1 Peter 2:14).
- Church leaders have the stick of "rebuking them sharply" (Titus 1:13) or failing that, by putting them out. That is how Paul dealt with Hymenaeus and Alexander, men he described as blasphemers, i.e. false teachers. Paul said he handed them over to Satan (1 Timothy 1:20). Handing someone over to Satan means putting him out of the church (1 Corinthians 5:2, 5). If rebuke and excommunication are the church's stick, the carrot is the joy of belonging to the church and sharing in the fellowship and spiritual privileges of Christians.
- Parents have the rod of discipline as their quite literal stick (Proverbs 22:15). The family also has the carrot of *belonging*. A godly family will be bound together with ties that are difficult to break. The prodigal son had fond memories of his father's house which drew him back when he finally came to himself.

The carrot and the stick, under God's providence, are enough to guarantee that a leader can control the flock God has given him. We can get back in control when we start using them.

How do you start? Two ways. First, you give special honor to those who deserve it, ignoring all the outcries from those who feel miffed at not getting the prizes they didn't earn. Just say to those people, as God did to Cain when he was upset because Abel's sacrifice was accepted and his wasn't:

> Why is your face downcast? If you do what is right, will you not be accepted? But if you do not do what is right, sin is crouching at your door; it desires to have you, but you must master it. (Genesis 4:6, 7)

Second, if you are a person in authority, you can start using the stick God gave you to use in your sphere. But even if you have no special position in the church and are not the head of a family, you have a secret weapon. If Christians start using it again, it will transform society. I'm talking about the Big Stick of godly peer pressure.

Walk Softly and Carry a Big Stick

Your opinion carries more influence than you think! In ages past, when Christians understood this, they were able to leaven all of America by simply encouraging godly behavior and cold-shouldering those who promoted and flagrantly practiced its opposite.

As usual, C. S. Lewis noticed both the problem (a society in which the vile are honored) and its solution (Christians exerting their proper influence) more than forty years ago. He wrote in an essay now included in a book entitled *Present Concerns* published by Harcourt Brace Jovanovich:

> The charge brought against us . . . will be that in cold-shouldering a man for his vices we are claiming to be better than he. This sounds very dreadful: but I wonder whether it may not be a turnip ghost [British for "a plausible illusion"].
>
> If I meet a friend in the street who is drunk and pilot him home, I do, by the mere act of piloting him, imply that I am sober. If you press it this implies the claim that I am, for that one moment and in that one respect, "better" than he. Mince it as you will, the mere brute fact is that I can walk straight and he can't. I am not saying in the least that I am in general a better man. Or again, in a lawsuit, I say I am in the right and the other man is in the wrong. I claim that particular superiority over him. It is really quite off the point to remind me that he has qualities of courage, good-temper, unselfishness and the like. It may well be so. I never denied it. But the question was about the title to a field or the damage done by a cow.
>
> Now it seems to me that we can (and should) blackball Cleon at every club and avoid his society and boycott his paper without in the least claiming any general superiority to him. We know perfectly well that he may be in the last resort a better man than we. We do not know by what stages he became the thing he is, nor how hard he may struggle to be

something better. . . . God knows, we are not saying that we, placed as Cleon, would have done better. But for the moment, however it came about—and let us sing *non nobis* ["not of us"] loud enough to lift the roof—we are not professional liars and he is. We may have a hundred vices from which he is free. But on one particular matter we are, if you insist, "better" than he.

And that one thing which he does and we do not is poisoning the whole nation . . . To prevent the poisoning is an urgent necessity. It cannot be prevented by the law: partly because we do not wish the law to have too much power over freedom of speech . . . The only safe way of silencing Cleon is by discrediting him. What cannot be done—and indeed ought not to be done—by law, can be done by public opinion. A "sanitary cordon" can be drawn round Cleon. If no one but Cleon's like read his paper, much less meet him on terms of social intercourse, his trade will soon be reduced to harmless proportions.

"This Town Ain't Big Enough for the Two of Us"

Jesus told His hearers to treat unrepentant sinners "like you treat a pagan or a tax collector." Tax collectors and pagans were treated pretty roughly in those days. They were about as popular as hail at a picnic. If a good Jew saw a prostitute on the street, he wouldn't stop and chat with her, he'd cross over to the other side. If, God forbid, the tax collector should try to horn his way in at a social function, everyone in the room would cut him dead socially.

We Americans know how to cut someone dead for wearing the wrong brand of designer jeans. Now we need to recover the fine social art of making a person actively practicing evil feel ashamed, and teach this art to our children. We are not rejecting the sinner. The minute he takes off his sin and leaves it outside, he can come in the room. We're just letting him know the way things are—this home, this church, and this nation just ain't big enough for Jesus and Satan!

If Adam and Eve had blackballed the serpent, we wouldn't even know what adultery and homosexuality and lying and stealing are. There would be no excuse for schools to teach Values Clarification because all values would be clearly understood and agreed to by all. Our first parents' fatal mistake was in not *silencing* Satan. They gave him time to speak.

Satan is always trying to distract us from protecting and building up the household of faith, starting with our own households. The only reason he ever succeeds is that we sometimes lose track of our main calling. Like the Israelites who wanted to trade God in for the cucumbers and leeks of Egypt, we sometimes miss out on the big picture.

Let's take a look now at God's big picture for us as individuals, households, and churches. It's outlined in the next chapter.

🍎 10 🍎

The Big Picture

Hell is not easily conquered; yet we have this consolation with us, that the harder the conflict, the more glorious the triumph. What we obtain too cheap, we esteem too lightly; 'tis dearness only that gives everything its value. Heaven knows how to put a proper price upon its goods . . .
Thomas Paine

Therefore, since we are surrounded by such a great cloud of witnesses, let us throw off everything that hinders and the sin that so easily entangles, and let us run with perseverance the race marked out for us. Let us fix our eyes on Jesus, the author and perfecter of our faith, who for the joy set before him endured the cross, scorning its shame . . .
Hebrews 12:1, 2

One of our family's favorite books is *The Hobbit* by J. R. R. Tolkien. It is a story about how a hobbit (a small, furry-footed, manlike creature) and thirteen dwarves went on a perilous journey to the Lonely Mountain to recover the dwarves' treasure from the dragon who had stolen it.

The book, in spite of Tolkien's strong dislike of allegories, is loaded with incidents that vividly illustrate principles of the Christian life. For instance, at one point on the dwarves' journey, they had been traveling through a gloomy and dangerous forest for quite a while and were beginning to wonder how far they had yet to go before they got out. So they sent Bilbo, as the smallest and lightest, up a tall tree to see if he could see the end of the forest.

Bilbo climbed to the topmost branches of the tree. After sight-seeing for a while, he remembered what he had come for and tried to catch sight of the edge of the trees. To his disappointment, all he could see was woods in all directions. His report to the dwarves discouraged them so much that they foolishly disobeyed the wizard Gandalf's order to keep to the path. As a result, the hapless dwarves were captured first by giant spiders (from which Bilbo rescued them) and second by the hostile King of the Elves.

Ironically, the dwarves were actually in a hollow not very far from the edge of the forest. Because the ground ahead was rising, Bilbo could not see over the edge.

Bilbo gave an inaccurate report to the dwarves because he didn't see the big picture. His view was limited to his immediate surroundings. If he had been able to fly and get a birds-eye view of their situation, he would have told a completely different story.

They Came, They Saw, They Fell

In Chapter Four, we saw that concentrating on short-term worldly advantages leads to falling for the lust of the eyes, the lust of the flesh, and the pride of life. Eve "saw" the fruit of the tree was nice to look at, good to eat, and desirable for making her wise. She and Adam enjoyed their choice for a few seconds . . . and they and their descendants have been suffering for it for thousands of years.

Adam and Eve missed out on the big picture. They didn't see how continuing to obey God, however unappealing the serpent made it seem at the present moment, would lead to good results in the end. They looked at the world through Satan's eyes, instead of through God's, and like the hobbit and his friends the dwarves, ended up missing the path.

The antidote, then, to Satan whispering, "If it looks like it will feel good, do it!" is to see your life and your choices as God sees them.

How *does* God see things? If God loves you and has a wonderful plan for your life, how can you find out what it is? What is Jesus' reason for asking us to deny ourselves and not give in to every passing desire?

Four Not-So-Easy Pieces

God has a plan for this world. The New Testament describes our place in that plan using four pictures:

- Erecting a building
- Serving as a soldier
- Competing as an athlete
- Working as a farmer

These four metaphors are four pieces of the big picture.

The World as a Demolition and Construction Project

The first metaphor is erecting a building. Just as with any construction project, the workers have to sweat at tearing down old structures found on the property and digging up the ground before building can begin.

Jesus described His ministry both as a tearing down and a building up. Jesus came to destroy the devil's work (1 John 3:8) and He came to redeem us from wickedness and prepare a people for Himself (Titus 2:14).

In one sense, both these jobs were finished at Jesus' death, when He cried, "It is finished!" as He paid the final price for the sins of His people and delivered us from Satan. In another sense Jesus continues the work through His Body, the church, as we evangelize and disciple the nations. The Great Commission which Jesus gave the church emphasizes both evangelism (preparing a people for the Lord) and discipleship (destroying the work of the devil in their lives and the lives of those they affect). Jesus says:

> Go and make disciples of all nations, baptizing them in the name of the Father and of the Son and and of the Holy Spir-

it, and teaching them to obey everything I have commanded you. (Matthew 28:19, 20)

Baptizing the nations is preparing a people for God. Teaching them to obey is destroying the work of the devil, first in their own lives, and ultimately in society as well.

Some people try to separate these two. One group says that the world is the devil's and thus a total loss, so the church should concentrate on evangelism. The other group says that Jesus wants us to take over society for Him and that this is the important thing. But these two good goals of evangelism and Biblical social change are not mutually exclusive!

Evangelism, if successful, will inevitably change society. In the early twentieth-century revival in Wales, all the taverns in one town had to close for lack of business because so many people became Christians. During and after the eighteenth-century Great Awakening, Christian statesmen like Oglethorpe and Wilberforce successfully led the British Parliament to eliminate child labor and slavery.

A pro-abortion Senator who gets saved and repents will change both his behavior *and* his vote in Congress. A judge who gets saved and starts upholding law and ruling justly in his court can do the devil's kingdom real harm, since graft, corruption, and favoritism are the devil's agenda.

On the other hand, destroying the works of the devil by living a Christian life in the world is pre-evangelistic. The Christian plumber who gets saved and lets his faith improve his work is doing pre-evangelism. He doesn't have to paint Bible verses on the pipes he replaces to do it, either! Simply by providing the best materials and excellent workmanship for his fee and by guaranteeing his work and cheerfully fixing anything that isn't right, he can help revive people's faith in honesty and integrity. Whether or not he gets to talk directly to his customers about Jesus, just by being honest and courteous he will help restore a Christian atmosphere to society.

Even your behavior at a four-way stop sign can make a difference. How courteous or rude you are can either give someone a lift or ruin their ride to work. (You need to be especially careful if you're sporting a "Jesus Saves" bumper sticker!) Your cheerfulness can give people a feeling of hope in this fallen world and make believing in God easier for them.

The Bible says you can't believe in what you have not heard, and it is likewise very difficult to believe in what you have never seen. A woman who has never met a faithful man finds it hard to believe in a faithful God. A child who has never received forgiveness and love finds it almost impossible to understand the nature of our merciful and loving God. At this very minute the church is filled with people who have serious spiritual problems because of the poor image their fathers gave them of God the Father—and there are even more who won't come near a church because of stumbling-blocks like this. Don't let anyone tell you that preaching is all there is to evangelism, when seeing Christianity in action is what makes the words make sense!

Drunkards and victims of childhood abuse do get saved, and we praise God for this. But how much better to come into the kingdom of God without having built up the bad habits and suffered through the bad experiences life offers through those who are doing the works of the devil! Insofar as our contacts with other people provide a nurturing, Christian atmosphere we are destroying the works of the devil, who would just love to make this world into Hell on earth.

This is the Army, Mr. Jones!

One of the great things about the Bible is the way it gives us varied snapshots of the Christian life, each of which contribute something to the big picture. If the first snapshot showed a workman in overalls intent on erecting a beautiful building, the second snapshot is that of a soldier in full armor defending that building. The New Testament in a number of places vividly compares being a Christian to enlisting in God's army. Paul writes to Timothy:

> Endure hardship with us like a good soldier of Christ Jesus. No one serving as a soldier gets involved in civilian affairs—he wants to please his commanding officer. (2 Timothy 2:3-4)

This picture piece adds an element of conflict and suffering to our Christian calling. We are not just working with inert materials, as in construction—materials like stone, wood, and bricks. We have to struggle against powerful spiritual forces. This requires both dedication and valor. We are at *war*, and this should make a whole lot of difference in how we handle ourselves.

It's Been a Hard Day's Fight

First, we must endure hardship. A soldier has to be ready to move out at a moment's notice at any hour of the day or night and in any weather. When he is in the field, he doesn't bring his feather bed with him. He sleeps on the ground in a tent at best. In Korea the troops slept many a night in water-filled foxholes. There are no steaks and gravy in the trenches. Rations are always plain and sometimes scant.

Right now in America we don't have to endure much hardship for Jesus' sake. Even so we should still be willing to put ourselves out, to stay up all night explaining the gospel to a seeker, to go out into a rainstorm to help a Christian brother or friend whose car broke down when we are the only person he could think of to call, to provide clothes for a family who have been burned out of their home, to rinse diapers, to skip meals, to lose sleep, to work hard . . . if our Commander-in-Chief commands us to. If persecution should break out in earnest, we should be willing to risk our lives, fortunes, and sacred honor for Jesus Christ.

We may not benefit directly in this world from our contribution to the war. That's why it's important to keep the big picture in mind. Think of the guy who covers a hand grenade with his body and saves a bunker full of men. He doesn't get to enjoy wearing the medal they pin on his chest, yet his contribution to the war still was great. Maybe those other men will go on and break the enemy line in a key spot, or take an important hill. But none of them would have been alive at all if not for his heroism.

Jimmy Stewart played the leading character, George Bailey, in the movie *It's a Wonderful Life*. The movie opens on

Christmas Eve with half the town individually praying for George, who is at the cracking point due to the machinations of old Mr. Potter, the town millionaire. On the very day the bank examiner came to look over the books, Mr. Potter stole some money that was supposed to be deposited into George's savings and loan association. Since the books can't possibly come out straight due to the missing deposit, George fully expects to be accused of embezzling and thrown in jail. This seems like the last straw to George, who has spent his life giving up every one of his earthly dreams for the sake of duty, seemingly without reward.

In the movie, an angel is sent down from Heaven to convince George that suicide (which would enable his family to cash in on his life insurance and avoid the scandal of his going to jail) is not the answer. The angel shows George what the town would be like if George had never been born. His brother, whom he saved from drowning as a boy, would be dead. All the men his brother saved by downing two enemy bombers in World War II before they could sink a troop transport would also be dead, since his brother wouldn't have been alive to save them. The old pharmacist whose mistaken prescription for medicine George refused to deliver would end up in jail for killing the patient and turn into a drunk. George's friend the taxi driver would have been divorced instead of happily married. George's uncle would have been in the insane asylum. One of the girls he knew would have become a prostitute instead of staying respectable. The whole town would have become a Times Square sin alley instead of the clean little town it was. And on and on. As the angel told a by-now repentant George Bailey, "You see, George, you really had a wonderful life!"

Nothing had changed in George's situation. He still had to go back to face a sheriff with a warrant for his arrest. But George now saw the big picture. He understood that, whatever happened to him, his sacrifices had been worthwhile.

Stepping Around a Sticky Situation

Second, a Christian soldier should not get entangled in civilian affairs. Garden catalogs market a product called "Tanglefoot."

Sometimes it comes as strips of material coated with a sticky goo. You place the Tanglefoot around the base of a plant, and bugs that try to climb up the plant get stuck.

In His parable of the farmer sowing the seed, Jesus pointed out that for some of us "life's worries, riches, and pleasures" choke out the Word of God in our lives, making us unfruitful (Luke 8:14). Worries, riches, and pleasures are like the Tanglefoot on the gardener's tree trunk. Any little bug that crawls into the Tanglefoot sticks right there and dies a miserable death. Any Christian who gets his eyes off the big picture and bogs down in chasing after riches and pleasures or worrying about himself will find himself stuck in Satan's web.

Isn't it true that our worries about the future and our quest for riches and pleasure are what is forcing us into the world's mold? We're starting to look exactly like the world because we're worried about and chasing after the same things they are. Don't we remember that Jesus said,

> Do not worry, saying, "What shall we eat?" or "What shall we drink?" or "What shall we wear?" For the pagans run after all these things, and your heavenly Father knows that you need them. But seek first his kingdom and his righteousness, and all these things will be given to you as well. (Matthew 6:31-33)

Isn't it about time that we started saying first, "Lord, here I am. What do You want me to do?" and then counting on *Him* to make it possible? As the Bible says, "Who serves as a soldier at his own expense?" (1 Corinthians 9:7). All our fretting and scheming and striving only serves to divert us from serving the Lord.

The Lord:	I have this job for you to do. (It may be having another baby, or looking after your children at home, or starting a Good News Club in your backyard, or taking in your old ailing mother.)
Us:	But I can't afford to do that! I'd have to give up my paycheck . . . or my wife's paycheck . . .

	or my chance for a promotion . . . or my dream of owning my own house. Sorry, Lord, send someone else.
The Lord:	*You* are the one I am calling. I can supply all your needs in Christ Jesus.
Us:	I won't believe it unless I put my hand in my wallet and see the money with my own eyes.

Let's end the dialog here. What the Lord would have to say next would be just too painful to repeat! What *can* He say to someone who doesn't believe that the King of the Universe who owns the cattle on a thousand hills can come through with a few dollars? Who gave Jesus Christ such a bad credit rating, anyway?

The problem, of course, is not that in our saner moments we don't believe that God can provide us with our daily bread. The problem is that we want so much more than daily bread! The solution is to remember that soldiers have to give up some of the nice things of life to achieve a better thing—winning the war!

"This Is Good and Pleases God"

Third, a good soldier wants to please his commanding officer. Soldiers *have* to obey their commanding officer or be court-martialled, but the C.O. is more pleased when his men obey because they have faith in him, when they trust that he knows the best thing for them to do.

It really helps to know that God *can* be pleased with us. It is probably no accident that the driest periods in church history, periods followed by widespread apostasy in the next generation, were times when preachers felt it their bounden duty to ceaselessly nag their hearers and never encourage them. So let's just briefly consider what does please God. (I encourage you to get a concordance and look up the words *please, pleases, pleased,* and *pleasing.* This is one Bible study that is sure to please!)

God is pleased by:

- Prayers for all men, and especially for rulers, that we may live unmolested and godly lives—1 Timothy 2:4
- Praise of Him—Hebrews 13:15
- Confessing the name of Christ—Hebrews 13:15
- Doing good and sharing with others—Hebrews 13:16
- Presenting our bodies to God as spiritual sacrifices (meaning letting Him do with our bodies what He will, rather than making an idol of our health or figures)—Romans 12:1
- Righteousness, peace, and joy in the Holy Spirit—Romans 14:17, 18

This is only a partial list. Notice how often faith and trust in God is implied by the items on this list. That is not surprising, because the Bible also lists some things that definitely displease God:

- Lack of faith—Hebrews 11:6
- Trying to please men rather than God—Galatians 1:10
- Being controlled by the sinful nature—Romans 8:8

Again, this is a partial list. The whole Bible tells us how to please or displease God. And God Himself tells us what pleases or displease Him by the witness of His Spirit. "There is no peace, says the Lord, for the wicked," but on the other hand, "You will keep in perfect peace him who trusts in you" (Isaiah 48:22, 26:3). Only the Christian soldier who is at war will ever know this peace.

It's How You Play the Game

The third snapshot in the big picture of the Christian life is the athlete straining to win a medal. The Bible uses the picture of an athlete to symbolize our need to train ourselves and to learn fair play. Paul used this illustration when he wrote to the Corinthians:

Do you not know that in a race all the runners run, but only one gets the prize? Run in such a way as to get the prize. Everyone who competes in the games goes into strict training. They do it to get a crown that will not last; but we do it to get a crown that will last forever. Therefore I do not run like a man running aimlessly; I do not fight like a man beating the air. No, I beat my body and make it my slave so that after I have preached to others, I myself will not be disqualified for the prize. (1 Corinthians 9:24-27)

This picture adds an element of self-control and striving to our picture. As soldiers we have to endure hardships, but hardship is part of a soldier's life over which he has no control. The life of an athlete is a life of self-inflicted hardship. As weightlifters say, "No pain, no gain." The athlete is training so that he can win a prize in a competition.

Our prize as Christians is salvation. Paul says that we must strive for salvation. Paul says elsewhere, "I press on to take hold of that for which Christ Jesus took hold of me. . . . Forgetting what is behind and straining toward what is ahead, I press on toward the goal to win the prize" (Philippians 3:12-14).

Paul obviously does not believe in the insurance-policy gospel. He beats his body to bring it into submission, he presses on, he strains toward his goal. Paul knows he's a Christian, but he still strives for the reward that God has promised to give him. But Paul is not a workaholic. We know he's not afraid of losing his salvation (Romans 8:35-39).

Paul knew how deceitful our human hearts are. He had known men who everyone thought were Christians, but who ended up exposed as apostates (1 Timothy 1:18-20). Paul was determined that he would not be one of them. "The way to make sure you can run the race to the end," Paul says, "is to make sure you are in shape."

How do you train for the salvation race? Maybe if you read your Bible and pray for eight hours every day, then you will be spiritually strong enough to finish the run. No, Bible reading is like eating, and praying is like talking strategy and getting the route straight with your coach. These are necessary to running a good race, but Paul is not talking about devotional exercises here. In order to gain strength for running you have to practice running. In order to get better at living the Christian life you have to practice living the Christian life.

You don't train for a marathon by running marathons. You practice for the big twenty-six-miler by running ten miles a day. You learn self-control in the big things by controlling yourself in the little things. Jesus says if you are faithful in the little things you will be faithful in the big ones.

Paul said he doesn't run aimlessly, or box at the air. He trains hard and purposefully. We likewise have to consciously train ourselves. When we see an opportunity for training, we should grab at it. When your four-year-old comes running into a room and stomps on your foot with his hard little shoe, that is an opportunity to learn patience and self-control. When the budget extends to either a new set of golf clubs or piano lessons for the children, but not both, this is an opportunity to learn Christian stewardship. Filling out your tax return is an opportunity for practicing honesty. Throwing away sweepstakes entries in the mail and passing up state lottery tickets in the supermarket are both good preparation for surviving a business trip to Las Vegas.

Want to know why the church today is so weak when facing the world? It's at least partially because we are passing up so many opportunities for training! We are supposed to prepare for church leadership, for example, by raising our own children successfully (1 Timothy 3:4, 5). Yet nothing is more common than to see Christian couples stopping their "planned" families at one or two children in order to have "more time for ministry"! On top of this add the deplorable tendency to ship the children off to day-care, nursery, baby-sitters, and preschool, and Christian parents hardly have any chance to get trained at all!

Thus the Farmer Sows His Seed

The fourth part of the big picture shows a farmer walking behind his plow. Paul says, "The hardworking farmer should be the first to receive a share of the crops" (2 Timothy 2:6).

This adds the last piece to the picture, the hope of a long-term reward.

What reward does the Christian farmer get? First of all, he receives his personal salvation. Second, he receives treasure in Heaven. Third, he has the joy of "bringing in the sheaves." As the Psalm says,

> He who goes out weeping,
>   carrying seed to sow,
> will return with songs of joy,
>   carrying sheaves with him. (Psalm 126:6)

Or, as Scripture puts it in another place, "Let us not become weary in doing good, for at the proper time we will reap a harvest if we do not give up" (Galatians 6:9).

Sometimes we can even have the joy of seeing our seed bear fruit for Jesus in this world. Psalm 128 says that if you "fear the Lord" and "walk in his ways" you will "eat the fruit of your labor." It then goes on to list some specific blessings:

- Your wife will be a fruitful vine within your house.
- Your children will be like olive shoots around your table.
- You may see the prosperity of Jerusalem (figuratively, the church in a prosperous and blessed state).

Psalm 112 also lists some specific blessings:

- Your children will be mighty in the land.
- Wealth and riches will be in your house (don't get too excited—this can figuratively refer to the spiritual wealth and riches we have in Christ!).
- You will look in triumph on your foes.

This last promise, that those of us who sow good seed for God will get to see His victory over our spiritual enemies, is repeated again and again in the Psalms. I do not believe we can spiritualize this promise away into merely a promise that we will see the doom of the wicked at the end of all things. It is intermixed with promises that nations will be subdued under Christ, a promise that has already partially come to pass in this age of the church.

What does the farmer hope for when he sows his seed? He should hope for nothing less than *revival!*

Heaven Came Down

Now it's time to take a look at the whole big picture. Imagine what the world would look like if Christian light and salt had its old-time oomph.

You walk in to work. Nobody there curses or uses the Lord's name in vain. If such an expression should slip out, the culprit blushes and apologizes. The *Playboy* centerfolds you used to see tacked up in the car shop are missing when you take in your car at lunch for a tuneup. Flipping through the Yellow Pages, you see that the first entry no longer is Abortion, and the ads for Escort Services and Massage Parlors have also mysteriously disappeared.

Driving home, you notice "For Sale" signs on bars all over town. Several of the bars have signs announcing a Christian bookstore is "Coming Soon" in that space. The sexy ladies you used to see draped across billboards everywhere have also been replaced by more wholesome promotional messages.

Reading your newspaper at home, you run across an editorial urging the readers to see God's hand in blessing and disasters. The headline articles are about *real* news, including the progress of the gospel in this and other lands, and no entertainment celebrity is even mentioned before page 78C. Crime is down, you notice as you flip through the paper, and Sunday church attendance is up. The big news story is that the federal budget not only balances but is in the black, with the excess going towards finally making some progress towards canceling the nation's debt. This budget-balancing has been made possible by the dismantling of hundreds of no-longer-needed bureaucracies. Workers from these bureaucracies are being offered retraining, but many of the women are simply deciding to settle down and work at home. Most of the remaining people laid off are planning to start their own businesses or joining up with the new ventures of others.

Finishing with the newspaper, you flip on the VCR. The networks, clinging grimly to their diet of sex, profanity, blasphemy, and violence, perished long ago. Now most people prefer videos to the remaining broadcast cable shows. Hot videos this season are "Testimony Tales," a series of dramatizations of real-life conversions from this and previous centuries, and "Tongues of Fire," a dramatization of the life of nineteenth-century Baptist preacher C. H. Spurgeon.

At dinner, your wife tells you that the public school building down the block has just been bought by a Christian school, and there's talk in your state about ending public education altogether as so few students are now served by it. "Then I guess we'd better give a few more dollars to the Christian Charity School Fund," you tell her. Since public schools were always the main conduits of illicit drugs, the revival in Christian education has also drastically reduced drug abuse in America. Youngsters are joining the churches in droves, further reducing the market for such drugs. What is left of public education looks more and more Christian, as school districts desperately try to compete with the powerful Christian school and home-schooling movements.

Is this some utopian dream? No, I am just reporting the way things *actually were* in America for more than a hundred years after our great revivals! With the exception of my little fantasy about post-revival video, each and every detail above is historically accurate. And I've even left out a lot of the best stuff: families restored, the promiscuous repentant, laws changed to actually protect the innocent, millions of Hell-bent sinners saved, and an outpouring of funds and prayers for Christian missions. Those revivals affected *all* areas of life, from fashion and dress to language and sexual mores.

We will never have Heaven on earth until Christ physically returns—but Heaven *can* come down and visit us!

Now, isn't that worth working and sacrificing for? Isn't it worth giving up the short-term pleasures the devil is tempting us with in order to have a part in bringing about such blessing for our neighbors, our children, and (should the Lord delay His physical return) our children's children?

Nowadays we are being tempted to believe that sowing the seed will have no long-term results—so why even bother? God's people are discouraged. "Just look at the state of the world," we tell each other. "Surely if everything's this bad we can't make any difference."

But Christians *can* make a difference—a lot bigger difference than most of us believe! Find out how we can transform this world in the next chapter.

11

The Transformers

*Our doubts are traitors,
And make us lose the good we oft might win,
By fearing to attempt.*
                                William Shakespeare

Do not conform any longer to the pattern of this world, but be transformed by the renewing of your mind. Then you will be able to test and approve what God's will is—his good, pleasing, and perfect will.
                                Romans 12:2

When Jesus touched a leper, He didn't get leprosy—he changed the leper! When Christians today touch the world, does the world get Christianity, or do we get spiritual leprosy?

As you saw in Chapter Three, Satan manipulated Eve into wanting to join his team, the in-crowd, by using peer pressure. He used innuendo, gossip, and lightly-veiled scorn to separate her from God and force them to go along with what he said. He tempted her with godhood. "You don't have to let God run the show; you can be like God just like me." Satan invited Adam and Eve to enter the Like-God Club. Why should they be the only people in creation who didn't have a membership?

Are Christians Different from Other People?

As we saw in Chapter Two, there is a teaching in the church that could be labeled "Struggle Theology." What it says is this: "Christians are just the same as non-Christians. In fact, you would be proud and arrogant to say you are any different from the worst non-Christian, since we all are sinners. Salvation has produced no supernatural miracle to make us different. We sin just as much and in just the same ways as unbelievers. The best that Christians can do, poor sinners that we are, is to weakly struggle with our sins. Christians, like non-Christians, need counselling, not preaching, to be delivered from their sins. In fact, it is highly doubtful that Christians even *can* have victory over any of their sins."

Are Christians just non-Christians with an eternal-life insurance policy? No, we're not! Paul didn't write "To the saints in Ephesus, failures in Christ Jesus." He didn't say in Romans 8, "We are more than conquered." He didn't say, "If any man is found in Christ, he is the same old creation. Behold, all things are just the same as they were." He didn't tell the Philippians to do everything without complaining and arguing so that they might become more or less blameless and somewhat pure children of God without many obvious faults in a crooked and depraved generation, in which they glimmered feebly like glowworms in the dusk. (My thanks to British writer Michael Greene for this last clever misquote!)

Paul did write to "the saints in Ephesus, the *faithful* in Christ Jesus." He told us that we "are more than conquerors." He said, "If any man is found in Christ, he is a *new* creation. Old things are passed away; behold, all things are become new." He told the Philippians that they were supposed to become "blameless and pure" (not more-or-less blameless and partially pure!), "children of God without fault in a crooked and depraved generation in which you shine like stars in the universe as you hold out the word of life" (Philippians 2:14, 15).

When you became a Christian, if you really did, then you were created over, born again. You have become a new creature, a different kind of human being, created for good works (Ephesians 2:10). Where before you were not able not to sin, you are now able not to sin. Where before you served yourself, now serving God and others is a joy. Where once you looked for the boundary between good and bad so you could walk the line, now you try to find the best and firmest path. The words the Bible uses for people like this are *faithful, overcomers, conquerors*. The Bible doesn't talk about just "struggling" with sin, but about *overcoming* it!

I'll grant that no Christian is perfect yet, but Christians, true Christians, ought to be constantly getting better. Old bad habits should be getting replaced with good habits. Sins which held us in unbreakable chains before should no longer have dominion over us. This is the Bible's picture of a regenerated man.

Dare to Be Different

Christians *are* different from non-Christians. The problem comes when we are afraid to admit we are different. No one wants to be made fun of. No one wants to be ignored. The in-crowd makes it clear that if you are going to act like a Christian they are not going to have anything to do with you.

You need boldness and courage to not only admit you are a Christian, but to be *pleased* that you are a Christian. If others ridicule you because you are not sophisticated, don't be tempted to pretend you are as cynical and immoral as them! Sophisticated means worldly-wise, well-versed in the things of the world. For a Christian, being called naive and unsophisticated, i.e. innocent, is a compliment. Consider the alternative!

On the other hand, Christians should not be different just for the sake of being different. We don't need to wear long white robes or have crosses tattooed on our chests. We don't want to be eccentric, which means "off center"; we want to be Christ-centered.

How can we strike the balance? How can we be different without being weird or self-righteous?

Will the Real World Please Sit Down?

The first rule for a Christian who wants to be different is: Don't be pragmatic or "realistic." If God tells you to do something, do it, whether your friends can see any reason for it or not.

God led my wife, Mary, and me to do many things our families thought were crazy. When we first became Christians in Connecticut, we had no one to tell us in person what we were doing. All we had was Christian books, our Bibles, and each other. Mary had been an agnostic feminist. I was brought up in a fringe group whose beliefs can be summarized best by listing what they don't believe in. We asked Jesus to become our Lord, but didn't understand Jesus' sacrifice at all.

When we started telling people about our salvation, we soon realized how little *we* knew about it. Finding a place where we could learn about God and the gospel became priority one. We were living right at the limits of our income already, so we couldn't afford to go anywhere and study on the weekends. Also, the only places we trusted were too far away.

We were in a dilemma. Our families had a simple, pragmatic solution: forget the whole thing. But God led us to a different solution. I would quit my job, we would sell our condominium, and we would go to seminary in St. Louis. Everyone thought we were nuts. They used adjectives like "irresponsible" and "stupid." But we have the testimony of the years since that God "exists and rewards those who earnestly seek him" (Hebrews 11:6).

We have to live our lives based on a firm belief in God's power, that God can perform what He commands us to do. If someone's view of reality doesn't include God and His power, *that* is unrealistic. God frustrates the plots of the wicked, because the wicked don't figure Him into them.

Boldness Without Compromise

The second rule for how to be different as a Christian is—never compromise. In the movie *Chariots of Fire* Eric Liddell's father correctly says, "Compromise is the language of the devil." Jesus said, "The gates of Hades will not overcome [the church]." Given this guarantee that our enemy will not overcome us, why should we compromise? Compromise is flirting with the devil.

Here are three examples of how, and how not, to avoid compromise: Ahab, David, and the apostles.

The Bad Example of Ahab. Ben-Hadad attacked the nation of Israel while Ahab was king. The first year he was routed, but he came again the next spring. He insulted God by saying, "Their gods are gods of the hills, so we'll attack in the plains." As a result, God again allowed Ahab to defeat the Aramean army. God even delivered Ben-Hadad up to Ahab.

Ahab, as was his custom most of the time, forgot to ask God what to do with his prisoner. Ben-Hadad came to Ahab in sackcloth, begging for mercy. Ahab played Mr. Gladhand and gave Ben-Hadad his life in return for some cities and a trade agreement.

God sent a prophet to Ahab. The prophet came disguised as an Israelite soldier. As Ahab passed, the prophet called out, "Your servant went into the thick of the battle, and someone came to me with a captive and said, 'Guard this man. If he is missing, it will be your life for his life or you must pay a talent of silver.' While your servant was busy here and there, the man disappeared" (1 Kings 20:39, 40). Ahab told him, "You have pronounced your own sentence." Then the prophet revealed himself to Ahab and delivered his message: "This is what the Lord says, 'You have set free a man I had determined should die. Therefore it is your life for his life, your people for his people'" (v. 42).

Ahab compromised with an enemy God had determined to destroy, and look what happened to him! Remember, Jesus came to destroy the works of the devil. We must not make deals with him.

The Good Example of David. David, king of Israel, decided to bring the ark of God to Jerusalem. In his zeal and joy, he leapt and danced before the Lord dressed in a white linen robe and an ephod. His wife saw him leaping and dancing in front of the ark of the Lord and she despised him in her heart. The minute she had the chance, she rebuked him for appearing in public without proper kingly attire. David answered, "It was before the Lord, who chose me rather than your father or anyone from his house when he appointed me ruler over the Lord's people Israel—I will celebrate before the Lord. I will become even more undignified than this, and I will be humiliated in my own eyes" (2 Samuel 6:21, 22).

David was doing the will and work of the Lord. He told his wife that if she thought this was bad, he was willing to be even worse for the sake of God.

Compromise says, "Oh, you object to this? Well, I'm sorry, I'll never do it again!"

Boldness says, "You object to this? I am doing this to serve God in Heaven. I will do so even more!"

The Good Example of the Apostles. We think of the apostles as being so bold, but even they prayed for boldness. Peter and John were arrested for healing a crippled man and preaching about Jesus. The authorities couldn't think of a fitting punishment for healing a cripple, so they threatened them and let them go. Peter and John reported to the rest of the believers in Jerusalem what had happened and they all raised their voices in prayer. They asked for *boldness* to speak the Lord's word. God gave it to them. The Spirit shook the house and filled them all and they "spoke the word of God boldly."

Learn to Laugh at Foolish Men

The third rule of how to be different is: Learn to laugh at foolish men. Some people feel like Christians should never laugh at anyone, but here are a couple of Scriptural examples of God's people giving foolishness the old hee-haw.

Elijah Laughs at the Prophets of Baal. The time for the great showdown had come. Elijah and the prophets of Baal were going to have it out on top of Mount Carmel (1 Kings 18). Elijah, the challenger, set the terms of the contest. Each side would lay out a sacrifice on its altar and call on its god. The god who sent down fire to consume the sacrifice would be acknowledged as the true God.

The prophets of Baal took the first turn. They started to chant, "O Baal, hear us! O Baal, hear us! O Baal, hear us!" The day wore on. After a while they must have sounded more like this: "O Baal, hear us? O Baal, hear us? Please, Baal, hear us!"

Elijah began to taunt them, "Shout louder! Surely he is a God! Perhaps he is deep in thought, or busy, or travelling. Maybe he is sleeping and must be awakened." Baal's prophets apparently took this to heart, because they shouted louder. They jumped on the altar. They cut themselves. But by evening, they still hadn't awakened any response.

Elijah's turn came next. To really humiliate Baal's prophets and show how much more powerful the true God is, he dug a trench around the altar and had men douse the sacrifice, the wood, and the altar until the trench was full. Now, if God considers it wrong to make fun of people, you would expect God to make Elijah sweat a little just to teach him a little humility. But God answered Elijah immediately when he prayed. Fire from Heaven consumed sacrifice, wood, altar, and water. The people, duly impressed, proclaimed the Lord to be God, and killed all the false prophets. God honored Elijah's mockery of Baal and his ridiculous prophets.

Jesus Derides the Pharisees. Jesus, who preachers so often describe as meek and mild as milktoast, derided the Pharisees for their customs. For example, "You strain out a gnat but swallow a camel." Think of that picture! Here is a Pharisee carefully pouring his broth through cheesecloth to make sure every gnat (a gnat is an unclean animal) is strained out. Meanwhile a camel, also an unclean animal, though somewhat easier to spot, has his foot in the bowl.

God Mocks the Wicked Kings. God Himself is a mocker—of the wicked. Psalm 2 says that God will laugh when the kings of the earth band together and think they can overthrow him.

This is not to say that all mockery is good. Proverbs paints the mocker as the worst scoundrel of all and holds out little hope for him. You flog a mocker only so that *others* can learn wisdom. But the mockers of the Proverbs are different from my examples above. Proverbs 3:34 calls them "proud mockers." Elijah was a humble mocker. It was easy for him to go from his mockery to prayer. In Proverbs 17:5 the mocker mocks the poor, in Proverbs 19:28 he mocks at justice, and in Proverbs 30:17 he mocks his father. On the other hand, God mocks proud mockers (Proverbs 3:34).

The difference between a righteous mocker and an evil one is:

1) The righteous mocker does it humbly; and

2) The object of righteous mockery is wicked or self-righteous men.

Laughter Makes Folly Evident to All

Mockery has its place. When men hold other men in bondage, whether through fear or display of supposedly superior wisdom, mockery is often the only way to break that hold.

The priests of Baal bound the people by fear. The people of Israel may have liked Baal's prophets or they may have detested them, but it didn't matter because they feared them. When Elijah ridiculed the prophets and got away with it, the people threw off their fear and killed the prophets.

The Pharisees held the people of Jerusalem enthralled by their great knowledge of the law and traditions. If a Pharisee said something was so, and all the other Pharisees agreed, that's the way it was. Jesus did recommend most of what the Pharisees taught, because much of it was straight from God's Old Testament law. But he had to show how ridiculous many of their rules were in order to keep the people from worshipping the rabbis more than God.

Laughter Destroys Stuffed Shirts.

One old series of children's books features a talking pig named Freddy and an upstate New York county full of talking animals. These books are just full of good solid common sense and morals and the entire Pride household recommends them highly. In one of these books, *Freddy the Politician,* the animals had formed the First Animal Republic and were holding their first elections. The candidates were Mrs. Wiggins the cow (for the freedom party) and a bird from Washington named Grover Cleveland (for the bureaucratic statist party). Grover got up at the animals' meeting and delivered a really high-faluting, impressive political speech, as he had learned to do while nesting in a tree on the White House lawn.

The birds all cheered furiously. Worried because the birds outnumbered the rest of the animals, the cat, Jinx, turned to Freddy and Mrs. Wiggins for inspiration. He asked:

"Can't you do anything?"
Freddy shook his head, but Mrs. Wiggins's broad face suddenly broke into a smile. "I can," she said. "Leave it to me." And suddenly she drew in her breath and opened her mouth, and let out a tremendous laugh with the full strength of her lungs. And believe me, when a cow laughs as loud as she can, you sit up and listen. . . .
The cheering faltered and died down.

When Grover objected to the interruption and ordered her out of the room:

At this some of the animals looked rather shocked, for Mrs. Wiggins was a highly respected member of the community. "Hey, hey," said Jinx. "Aren't we going to laugh in this new republic if you're president?"
"Laughter," said Grover, "has its place. I should be the last to deny it. But its place is not in government. It is a destructive element."
"Destroys stuffed shirts," said old Whibley [the owl] in a loud voice. "And a good thing, too."

Laughter Destroys the Doctrines of Stuffed Shirts. Many so-called "experts" try to convince us that God's Word is no good for today. As long as you take them seriously, you are vulnerable to their false teaching. But when you can laugh at their folly, you know you have been immunized against it!

One of my Old Testament professors in seminary, J. Barton Payne, had an irrepressible sense of humor. He told us this amusing story about a naive student and a theologically-liberal professor at a liberal seminary.

> ### The Seminary Student and the Liberal Professor
> A young man who had never read the Bible got saved and immediately applied to seminary. His first day there, he was assigned to read through the book of Exodus. Soon he rushed into his professor's office all excited, crying, "Professor! A miracle! A miracle!"
>
> The professor, after calming the student down enough so he was coherent, asked, "Now what is this miracle?"
>
> The student answered, "God parted the waters of the Red Sea so the whole nation of Israel could cross on dry ground!"
>
> The professor, like his liberal colleagues, didn't believe in any such miracle. Reminding himself of the standard unbelieving response to the Red Sea miracle, he patiently answered, "That was the Reed Sea. The Reed Sea is only six inches deep. So you see that wasn't so great a miracle after all, was it?"
>
> Somewhat crestfallen, the student went back to his reading. However, a short time later he was back all excited again.
>
> "Professor! Professor! An even greater miracle! *God drowned the entire Egyptian army in six inches of water!*"

After hearing that story, no way would any student in that class buy the "Reed Sea Instead of Red Sea" fable! The folly of that little dig at God's truth had, in the Bible's language, "become evident to all" (2 Timothy 3:9).

Laughter Drives Out Fear

Foolish doctrines are stripped naked by a gale of holy laughter. But what about foolish plots and schemes? Even Christians have been known to quail a little at the thought of a major worldly conspiracy (Psalm 2). Shouldn't we be afraid of a coalition with all the nations of the earth united against God and His Messiah and, of course, against the Messiah's church?

God doesn't think so. He laughs them to scorn. Then He rebukes them and terrifies them.

As I am writing this, my wife, Mary, and my youngest son Franklin (age 1½) are eating breakfast in the kitchen. My son got angry because his mother made him put his puzzle on the floor instead of on a chair. "I'm mad!" he fumed. Mary verified that she had heard him correctly by repeating, "You're mad?" Then she laughed—not a nasty laugh, but an amused laugh at how Franklin was already learning to express his feelings like a grown-up. Our small son's anger didn't terrify her.

Neither does the impotent rage of a whole world full of people terrify God. We should follow His example, laugh at the posturings of mere men, and go about God's business without fear. When Satan, the stuffed shirt of stuffed shirts, starts casting doubts and fears our way, remember the power of the Lord and remember Mrs. Wiggins, and laugh.

Viva la Différence

We know we *are* different because we are Christians, but what good does it do?

Being different is good because being different makes a difference. Christians are the salt and light of the world. Salt is different from meat, and that is as it should be, because salt seasons meat and salt preserves meat. Meat won't season itself. If the salt becomes just like the meat, it's useless as salt. Light drives away darkness. Darkness can't drive away itself. "If then the light within you is darkness, how great is that darkness" (Matthew 6:23).

Being different is also good because it pleases God. God's constant refrain throughout the middle chapters of Leviticus is, "Be holy, because I am holy" (Leviticus 11:44, 45, 19:2, 20:7, 26). God called Israel "A kingdom of priests, and a holy nation" (Exodus 19:6). Israel was to be a people set apart for God. God wanted them to be different from the nations around them, and God gave them laws to ensure that they would stay that way. He gave them circumcision. He gave them special dietary laws. He gave them laws against eating blood. He gave them laws against marrying close relatives. All these made Israel different from their neighbors.

Peter renews the refrain for Gentile Christians in his first letter: "But you are a chosen people, a royal priesthood, a holy nation, a people belonging to God" (1 Peter 2:9). God wants us also to set ourselves apart from the people around us. But, where Israel was a distinct nation, Christians are spread throughout the nations. Where God gave Israel circumcision as a physical sign of their uniqueness, our circumcision is circumcision of the heart (Romans 2:29). Where Israel had their law inscribed on tables of stone, we Christians have that same law inscribed on our hearts by the Holy Spirit.

You Can't Win If You Don't Run!
In the movie *Chariots of Fire* one big scene is the matchup between the two fastest men in Great Britain, Harold Abraham of England and Eric Liddell of Scotland. Abraham, surprised at Liddell's speed, commits the cardinal sin in short-distance running: he turns his head near the end of the race to see whether he or Liddell is ahead. That costs him a fraction of a second and he loses the race.

Abraham had never been beaten before. After the race, he sits in the gallery totally discouraged, going over and over the race in his mind. His girlfriend tries to encourage him, but Abraham is determined to feel sorry for himself. In his bitterness he says he would quit running. When his girlfriend tries to rebuke him for his foolishness, he bursts out, "If I can't win, I won't run." She snaps back, "If you don't run, you can't win."

When you dare to compete rather than cooperate with the world, you *can* win. The gates of Hell can't prevail against you. You have Jesus' guarantee that all power in Heaven and on earth has been given to Him, and He will be with you even till the end of the age. If God is with us, who can be against us? One Christian doing the work of God can stand against the world and win.

Athanasius Contra Mundum
Back in the days that schoolboys routinely studied Latin, one of the famous Latin expressions they learned was *Athanasius*

contra mundum. This phrase means that if the world is against Athanasius, then "let Athanasius be against the world."

Who is Athanasius and why was he against the world? The story can encourage us today.

During the time Athanasius (A.D. 297?-373) was bishop in Alexandria, Egypt, a man called Arius arose preaching, as the Jehovah's Witnesses do now, that the Son and the Holy Spirit are subordinate to the Father, and that in fact the Son was the first created being. Athanasius preached and wrote against Arius and as a result was exiled five times during his twenty-five years as bishop. He felt like he was the only one in the world who believed as he did, thus his *Athanasius contra mundum* quoted above. But he persevered until his teachings were vindicated at the Council of Nicea in 325 A.D.

Athanasius' teaching wasn't popular for many years, but he knew he was right. He held out against all the peer pressure and persecution the world could dish out and he won! The leaders of the fourth-century church rejected Arianism. The creed they drafted is still used more than 1600 years later in the liturgies of many Christian churches. That's a lasting contribution!

Dewey Contra Christendom

You may think, "Well, that's all right for some great Christian hero of times past, but one man today can't change the course of history." Let's just briefly look at one man who did—a modern Arius who significantly changed the course of our nation for the worse.

John Dewey joined the faculty at the University of Chicago in 1894, and two years later started his now-famous Laboratory School. The idea of this school was to take normal kids and subject them to new "scientific" educational ideas based on a belief in man as an evolved monkey. A few years later than that, he moved to Columbia Teachers College and began the task of discipling others in his ideas. Since Columbia was a degree-granting institution, his disciples left not only saturated with Dewey's doctrines but armed with impressive-looking credentials. These graduates, in the words of education author

Samuel Blumenfeld, "fanned out across America to become deans and professors at other teachers' colleges and superintendents of entire public school systems."

Once in place, these men acted like an educational mafia, pushing for "reform" of local school government, such reform consisting of replacing elected officials with "experts." And who was more expert than the grads of dear old Columbia Teachers? As more and more of these Dewey disciples entered positions of influence, the prestige of a Columbia degree increased even more, and even *more* disciples got influential posts. All these men without exception crusaded for Dewey's agenda—Socialist education designed to destroy the old Christian values of responsibility, individuality, and the fear of the Lord and instill Dewey's personal beliefs, known today as Humanism. For, after all, John Dewey was perhaps the biggest shaker and mover behind the original 1933 Humanist Manifesto, signed by him and thirty-three others.

Sam Blumenfeld's book *NEA: Trojan Horse in American Education* follows this tale in harrowing detail, and shows how the National Education Association, the largest public school teachers' union and the most powerful lobby in America, took up Dewey's cause and still crusades for it today. From the replacement of phonics with look-say, to opposition to creationism, to the teaching of contraception, to homosexuality as an "alternative lifestyle," the NEA echoes Dewey straight down the line. What has happened to the public schools, and through them, to all America, in terms of the slide from Christian morality to pagan barbarism, can largely be traced directly to the efforts of this one man, Dewey.

Was Dewey rich? No. Did he have important social connections? Not really. Did he have great numbers behind him? Not at first. Others were also rebelling against the Christianity of their fathers, but they were by no means a majority, or even a significant minority. Throughout American history some people can always be found who are rebelling against God and teaching strange doctrines, but never before had they taken over the country! What Dewey did was to *inspire his followers with a goal* and to *believe in his goal*. He organized them. He promoted his movement. He didn't say, "Hey, look, almost all Americans would consider what we are teaching here to be nuts. We can't ever hope to have serious influence." He dared to be different (in a bad way) and moved all of society in his direction.

Move It or Lose It!

Why do we Christians today so often act like losers? Why do we so often assume that we will never make a difference, no matter what we do? Why do we so often tone down our message because we are afraid people will consider it too far-out? Why do we consult the polls instead of the Lord? It's shameful, but true—the Lord's enemies often have more courage for their cause than we do. Consider Dewey. Consider also, to get a bit closer to home, the homosexual lobby. Who would have thought, twenty years ago, that American society would ever accept homosexuality as a good and OK way to act? If ever a minority had all the deck stacked against them, the homosexuals did. What they do is disgusting and, according to the Bible, sinful. It is against natural law, man's law, and God's law. But a few determined homosexual and pro-homosexual crusaders who were willing to bear ridicule led the whole movement into the American mainstream.

If homosexuals can be this up-front about their difference, can't Christians? When we act or sound really different than those around us, at first we will be ridiculed. That comes with the territory. But if we keep acting different with *boldness,* human nature will lead people to become used to our ideas. They will no longer sound so strange. This is what happened with the homosexuals, and what is now happening with other sins struggling to swim into the mainstream. The oftener you hear an idea, the harder it is to be shocked by it. Well, that works for Christian ideas, too—ideas like salvation through the blood of Jesus Christ and the need for holy living—that sound strange to modern men.

The problem is that only *one* set of ideas—the wrong set—is being proclaimed boldly today. While we Christians whisper, the opposition shouts! We can't use their strong-arm tactics, but we *can* at least show as much confidence in our God as they have in their idols. Then let the best idea and the strongest God win—and I have an idea who it will be!

Christians *can* transform culture—not on our own, but with the Holy Spirit's power. But first we need to be transformed ourselves! Today some wrong attitudes towards God are hampering the church and weakening our work of evangelizing and discipling. We'll take a look at these attitudes, and how to correct them, in the next chapter.

🍎 12 🍎

Scared to Life

*He has sounded forth the trumpet that shall never call retreat;
He is sifting out the hearts of men before His judgment seat:
O be swift, my soul, to answer Him! be jubilant, my feet!
Our God is marching on.*
   Julia Ward Howe, "The Battle Hymn of the Republic"

For great is the Lord and most worthy of praise; he is to be feared above all gods.
                                            1 Chronicles 16:25

"I don't get no respect!" This is comedian Rodney Dangerfield's complaint. His whole routine is a series of variations on this theme. No respect from his kids. No respect from his wife. Audiences love it, because deep down each of us knows he has had his moments when the world didn't exactly shower him with respect, either!

Rodney Dangerfield isn't the only one who don't get no respect. God is the creator of the universe, but what kind of respect does that get Him? Most men today either ignore Him or deny He exists. Mythical Mother Nature gets more respect for what happens in creation than God does! Our modern ethicists don't even pay lip service to the God whose moral law has been the basis for ethics in the West for almost twenty centuries. If you told an American teenager that he should fear God you would get only a blank stare or, "Man, you're crazy!" in return. God just don't get no respect.

Adam and Eve Lose Respect for God . . . And Painfully Find it Again

In Chapter Two I showed how Satan gave Adam and Eve a case of the squishies. God had said, "You are free to eat from any tree in the garden; but you must not eat from the tree of the knowledge of good and evil, for when you eat of it you will surely die" (Genesis 2:16, 17). That was firm ground for them to stand on. As long as they feared the Lord's punishment, they wouldn't eat.

Then Satan came along to muddy the waters. He said God had lied when He said they would surely die. "God is bluffing," said Satan. "He is trying to scare you two away from the tree because He doesn't want you to eat the fruit and become like Him."

All of a sudden Adam and Eve were on squishy ground. They had been given conflicting stories and had no personal knowledge of the tree to help them decide whether God or the serpent was giving them the straight scoop. The decision they made could be based only on the character of the witnesses. Would they believe God, or would they believe Satan? And, if they believed God, did they fear Him enough to obey Him?

We know how it turned out: Eve believed Satan, and Adam, though he believed God, didn't obey Him.

Adam should have known better. When Adam first awoke, God was there. God placed him in the garden. God brought the animals to Adam to be named. God created Eve. God walked with Adam and Eve in the garden. They knew God. Why should they follow the word of that snake, Satan? Adam listened to Satan because Satan was playing his tune. Adam wanted to eat the fruit, but had been afraid to. Now Satan's rationalization and Eve providing him with an excuse by eating the fruit herself overcame Adam's fear of God. He no longer treated God like He was worthy of respect. He defied God and ate the fruit himself.

Adam's newfound boldness was short-lived. After he and Eve had eaten the fruit, when they heard God coming for His evening walk the fear of the Lord took on new meaning for them. They discovered very quickly that God definitely was worthy of respect. Adam and Eve now had learned something the hard way. They had discovered the beginning of wisdom—but not the way Satan had promised.

Is It Wrong to Fear the Lord?

The book of Proverbs tells us that the fear of the Lord is the beginning of wisdom (Proverbs 8:10). It is not fashionable nowadays to talk about fearing the Lord. Some people have even taught that being afraid of God is sinful. They quote John:

> God is love. Whoever lives in love lives in God, and God in him. In this way, love is made complete among us so that we will have confidence on the day of judgment, because in this world we are like him. There is no fear in love. But perfect love drives out fear, because fear has to do with punishment. The one who fears is not made perfect in love. (1 John 4:16-18)

A casual reading of these verses says that these people are right. John says that if we fear, we are not perfect in our love and therefore we are sinning. Let's compare this with the rest of the Bible.

Proverbs speaks for the whole Old Testament when it says that fearing the Lord is the beginning of wisdom (Proverbs 8:10). God wanted the nation of Israel to be a God-fearing people (Deuteronomy 6:13). David, a man after God's own heart, feared the Lord and tells us to fear Him also (Psalm 34:9). He complains that the wicked have no fear of God (Psalm 36:1). God says through Isaiah, "The Lord Almighty is the one you are to regard as holy, he is the one you are to fear, he is the one you are to dread" (Isaiah 8:13). This is only five verses out of almost a hundred telling us to fear the Lord.

That was the Old Testament. How about the New Testament? Jesus said we should fear God (Luke 12:4, 5). Paul says he knows what it means to fear the Lord (2 Corinthians 5:11). Peter exhorts us to live our lives here in reverent fear (1 Peter 1:17). And there are other verses encouraging us to fear the Lord in the New Testament as well, including some from the pen of John himself in Revelation (Revelation 14:7, 15:4, 19:5).

I rest my case. We are supposed to fear the Lord.

Fear of Frying

But what about 1 John 4? John was talking about one specific fear only—the fear of *condemnation by God* at the final judgment. Note his reference to "hav[ing] confidence on the day of judgment." This is the first of three kinds of fear of God that the Bible talks about.

Obviously those who are living in God and "God in them"—the born-again—do not need to suffer from this fear. Perfect love does, as John says, drive out this "fear of the Lord" that is the mere beginning of wisdom.

Fear of frying—that is, fear of spending eternity in Hell—may be simply the beginning of wisdom, but that does not mean it is not tremendously important. Jesus spent more time talking about Hell than about Heaven while He was on earth. Any evangelistic or doctrinal preaching worthy of the name *must* include description of the "wrath that is to come."

The Testimony of the Bible. I would like to mention at this point that the testimony of both the Bible and history is definitely on the side of those who plead with their hearers to avoid God's just judgment.

The entire message of Old Testament prophecy could be summarized as, "Obey God and be blessed or disobey and get wiped out." Prophets spoke of the Messiah as the one who could save us from judgment, not as some kind of spiritual band-aid sent to save us from disease.

In the New Testament age, John the Baptist, Jesus, and the apostles all left strongly-worded warnings of the fiery judgment of God. They warned again and again of *unquenchable fire* and *outer darkness* where there is *weeping and gnashing of teeth.* See Matthew 3:7-12 and 8:12, for example.

The Testimony of History. Now think of the greatest preachers in church history, men whose messages sparked countrywide revivals. We're talking about *real* revivals here, the kind with fruit that lasts, not the kind where those who come forward to "decide" for Christ are nowhere to be found three months later! Preachers of this world-shaking caliber like John and Charles Wesley, George Whitefield, Jonathan Edwards, and C. H. Spurgeon *all* preached searing messages about hellfire.

Let's take just two examples: Jonathan Edwards, who is generally considered the best American theologian, and C. H. Spurgeon, the best English-speaking preacher of all time.

Jonathan Edwards preached the gospel for years, but revival broke out when he preached his famous sermon, *Sinners in the Hand of an Angry God.* In this sermon, Edwards spoke of sinners as loathsome spiders suspended over the pit of hell, the only thing holding them up being a thread held by the God they offended. His hearers, rather than berating him for failing to affirm their self-esteem, repented by droves.

C. H. Spurgeon had similar results from his sermon, *Turn or Burn.* Although, like Edwards, Spurgeon could preach the love of God most meltingly, he also knew that his hearers needed to be scared to life. They needed the "beginning of wisdom"—the fear of God's judgment—to shock them into seeing how much God hates their sins. Only those who know God hates their sins and who come to hate those sins also can ever get saved. As Jesus said, He did not come to call the righteous, but sinners (that is, those who know they are sinners and hate themselves for it) to repentance.

Fear of frying is for those outside Christ, as the Apostle John points out. But does that mean those in Christ have nothing at all to fear?

The answer you give to that question depends on whether you think you are perfect or not. John said that *perfect* love casts out fear. This is true. Those who are living in the center of God's will have nothing to fear.

However, the Bible tells us of two remaining kinds of fear of the Lord that apply to Christians: *fear of spanking* and *fear of displeasing God.*

Fear of Spanking

We all are, or should be, familiar with the passage in Proverbs 3:11, 12, repeated in the book of Hebrews, that tells us God spanks his children:

> My son, do not make light of the Lord's discipline,
>   and do not lose heart when he rebukes you,
> because the Lord disciplines those he loves,
>   and punishes everyone he accepts as a son.
>   (Hebrews 12:5, 6)

As that passage goes on to say, if God does not discipline us, we are not even His children!

As that passage also goes on to say, it is possible to make light of the Lord's discipline. That is exactly what is happening today. We are asked to believe that God is too tenderhearted to ever cause us any pain. He is simply a spiritual psychiatrist whose job is to comfort us!

Those who believe this message are taught to ignore or deny God's discipline. They are told it is wrong to tremble before God . . . after all, he is our pal and buddy!

God is not our pal. He is our Father. He befriends us in the same way a very powerful, important man might befriend us, not by coming down to our level but by pulling us up towards his. And part of the way he does this is by spanking us.

Now, as any good mom or dad will tell you, a child who does not fear spankings is a child it is impossible to teach. The child may get spanked often or seldom, but his spankings only do him good when he wishes to avoid receiving another spanking for the same offense. His bottom has got to give him the message, "Hey, please, quit disobeying Mom and Dad and acting up. I don't ever want to go through this again!"

Many of us are spiritually sick and weak and some of us have died because we refuse to admit God has the right to chasten us and because we refuse to learn anything from His chastening when it comes. When we start catching on to the fact that the events in our lives don't just "happen" we can learn from God's testing and discipline.

Fear of Displeasing God

Once we get wise enough to fear God's spankings, we are ready for the next step—to fear displeasing God simply because we love Him and want to please Him.

Spiritual spankings teach us to see ourselves and the world from God's point of view. We start understanding how our sins grieve God. We become miserable when we sin, not because we fear Hell or because we fear discipline, but because we have offended our loving Father. The thing we fear most is not His arm of punishment, but the loss of His pleasure in us.

Psychologists today teach us never to withhold eye contact from our children, no matter what they do, lest they feel unwanted and unloved. The Bible disagrees with this teaching, since God Himself uses this form of discipline on His wayward children. He withholds "the light of his countenance" from those who displease Him. And this is the most devastating discipline of all for the mature Christian.

The Psalms, our prayer-book, are filled with pleadings that God will "look upon us" and "lift up the light" of His face upon us. When God is with us, smiling upon us, who can be against us?—but when God frowns on us, it should make our insides quiver. What could be worse than losing that wonderful peace and joy in Christ? What could be worse than having Father displeased with us? You who are spiritual know what I mean!

"They Call Us Mellow Jello" . . . Quite Rightly

But, to be perfectly honest, many Christians today hardly fear the Lord at all. We have become so mellowed out that we find it nearly impossible to believe that God could ever frown on us, no matter what we do. After all, since babyhood we have grown up in a society where as long as you have a good excuse you can literally get away with murder. Parents negotiate with their rebellious offspring rather than spanking them. In school, children are taught that they are super-special beings who deserve the fawning attention of the adult world. When you read your newspaper or watch the TV news you discover that the only sins left in the modern world are apartheid and stockpiling nuclear weapons. Even Christian preachers too often downplay the seriousness of sin and the Lord's heavy hand in dealing with it, making comments like "AIDS is not a judgment on homosexuals" (it is maybe a heavenly benediction instead?).

We can get that feeling of respect for God by meditating on what the Bible says about Him.

Worthy of Respect for His Power

God is worthy of respect for His awesome *power*. We think of fusion atomic bombs, the most powerful force man is able to unleash, with awe and fear. Yet the explosive energy in one thunderhead is more than that. Think of the power of the volcano Krakatoa when it exploded. The sound of that explosion was heard on the other side of the world. Think of the power of a tidal wave or an earthquake or a flood or a tornado. All of these are controlled by the hand of God.

When Babylon was attacking Israel, God through Jeremiah repeatedly threatened a triumvirate of disasters: plague, famine, and sword (Jeremiah 21:7, 9, 24:10, etc.). Would I be unreasonable to suggest that since God once had these in His arsenal, and God never changes, that He still has them? If He used these things once to destroy a faithless nation, couldn't He use them again?

Plagues. Take plagues, for example. Concern is high over the AIDS epidemic. But AIDS is not the only plague to hit the U.S.A. in the 1980s! We've had toxic shock. We have herpes. We have chlamydia. We have a whole host of pandemic illnesses spread from day-care child to day-care child. AIDS is merely the most dangerous of them and is getting the most media attention.

Some outspoken preachers have told us that AIDS, and I assume the rest, are not judgments from God. They claim that though God did strike nations with plagues in the Old Testament, He no longer does that. Since New Testament times, they say, God does not deal with nations the same way He did before Christ. I don't remember them using any Bible verses to substantiate their claims.

The book of Revelation throws a monkey wrench into their theory. Revelation is a book of prophecy related to the church age, i.e. post-New Testament. Chapters 15 and 16 tell of the pouring out of the seven vials, described as the seven last plagues, after which the wrath of God is spent. When will these plagues happen? I don't know, but this I do know—Revelation is not talking about the time *before* Christ Jesus! If God can talk about bringing plagues sometime in this age, then He can do it anytime. The rules haven't changed.

Sword. The same argument applies to the sword. God can still use the arm of man to carry out His judgment. How easy it would be, for example, for an apostate America to be bombed or threatened into total subjection by the USSR! I am not saying this necessarily will happen. But if it ever does, be sure of this—God, not the Russians, pulled the trigger.

Famine. And speaking of famine, have you noticed how dry and hot the weather has been? God doesn't have to ever let it rain on Texas, if He is displeased with Texas. Nor does He have to let it rain on Missouri, or Kansas, or southern California, for that matter. The famines in Africa and other places are not mere natural phenomena, but rather an invitation from the Lord to warn the people in those countries to "flee the wrath to come." Similarly, the droughts in America are God's first warning shots across the bow reminding us to slow down and remember just who is running things here.

Acts of God or Random Chance?

Secular scientists snow us with plausible theories to explain away God's hand in judgment. They have Cycle Theories (economic depressions and physical disasters just occur in natural cycles) and Nature-Lover Theories (industrial pollution causes every disaster) and more other theories than I can take time to name. What all these theories have in common is simply that they ignore the spiritual causes of disasters, which the Bible says are real and to be reckoned with. Pharaoh's magicians did the same thing. "Not to worry, Pharaoh. We know what causes these frogs all over the place. We can do the same thing." Good job, fellows—although it would have been more to the purpose to get rid of the frogs, if you could.

Some modern preachers concur in stripping God of his power. Ignoring the fact that even secular insurance policies talk about "acts of God"—e.g., tornadoes, hurricanes, and floods—they assert that God does not bring disasters. Who *does* bring them, then? Or are the humanists right, and everything that happens to this world has a strictly materialistic source?

The Bible has the answer, summed up in this verse:

> When disaster comes to a city, has not the LORD caused it?
> Surely the Sovereign LORD does nothing without revealing
>   his plan to his servants the prophets. (Amos 3:6, 7)

Preaching the God Who Acts

Real prophets (today, preachers) know how to interpret the signs of the times. They acknowledge the hand of God in history, even in current history. They do not attribute every awful occurrence to the devil as the ultimate source (thus making the devil seem more powerful than he is), or to the schemes and plots of wicked men. They do not assign the credit for blessings to Mother Nature or Lady Luck, either!

God's power is not confined to bringing disasters on rebellious people, churches, cities, and nations. He can and does bring great blessings. We tend to take the blessings we have for granted, but the Bible says that all good things come from God (James 1:17).

Satan has no power to create or distribute blessings, and he has no real power of his own to bring disaster. Even the devil has to pray for what he wants. See for example the book of Job, or how the demons Jesus cast out of the Gadarene demoniac had to beg Him not to send them to the abyss.

God may occasionally use Satan as His tool for punishing wicked men or for "spanking" his children (see 1 Corinthians 5:5 and 1 Timothy 1:20), but Satan never gets to conduct business on his own without the permission of God. How much less does "the weather" or some new virus strain act on its own!

In every great revival, the evangelists were not shy to attribute great blessings and great disasters to the hand of God. People listened, came under the fear of the Lord, repented, and were saved in great numbers. May God send us more men like this today!

Worthy of Respect for His Character

God is worthy of respect for His awesome power, and even we Christians should "live our lives as strangers here in reverent fear" (1 Peter 1:17). But our respect for God shouldn't be based entirely on fear. The fear of the Lord is, after all, only the *beginning* of wisdom. Our respect for God should be based also on love of God's character. "Perfect love drives out fear" (1 John 4:18).

God is not all fire and wrath, and especially not for Christians. God is love. All men experience God's love, even those who are His enemies. Jesus tells us:

> Love your enemies and pray for those who persecute you, that you may be sons of your Father in heaven. He causes his sun to rise on the evil and the good, and sends rain on the righteous and the unrighteous. (Matthew 5:44, 45)

Even the "evil" and the "unrighteous" feel the love of God in a general way, whether they know God or not. But we who believe in Him know His love in a special way.

Jesus says, "Greater love has no one than this, that he lay down his life for his friends" (John 15:13). The Apostle Paul says the same thing even more poignantly:

> You see, at just the right time, when we were still powerless, Christ died for the ungodly. Very rarely will anyone die for a righteous man, though for a good man someone might possibly dare to die. But God demonstrates his own love for us in this: While we were still sinners, Christ died for us. (Romans 5:6-8)

Can't you respect a God who will do this?

Great Is the Lord, and Most Worthy of Praise

Summed up in God's love is a host of other character traits. For example, think of God's *humility*. Yes, God is humble! God's humility astonished King David. He wrote, "When I consider your heavens, the work of your fingers, the moon and the stars, which you have set in place, what is man that you are mindful of him, the son of man that you care for him?" (Psalm 8:3, 4). How amazing that the Most High God should have anything to do with mere men! Members of the aristocracy in England won't associate with the common men on the streets. But God in Heaven will! Isn't that wonderful!

That we lived long enough to be saved is an example of God's *mercy*. Beware, if you are ever tempted to ask for justice from the Lord. Justice would have been the death of you before you got out of the cradle.

Israel tried God's *patience* over and over again. And God came through and showed His *kindness* over and over again. They complained about the bitter waters of Marah and God sweetened them. They complained about being hungry and God fed them with manna and quail. They complained about their lack of water at Horeb and God gave them water from a rock. Only after their complaining turned to rebellion did God become angry.

But we don't have to look as far away as Israel for examples. I am sure many of you have had times when you tried God's patience and God responded with kindness. That happened to my wife, Mary, and me just after we had our first baby, during the tough time when the little one was getting up three and sometimes four times a night.

Mary was getting more and more exhausted. One day she was so tired she gave in to resentment for God "never" letting her get enough sleep. I felt the same way, so I wasn't much help in calming her down. Her distress kept her up so late that she "just knew" the baby would wake up as soon as she went to bed. She "knew" God would give her a miserable night to punish her for getting so angry. Still, to make the best of a bad situation, she went to bed. That night the baby slept from midnight till eight in the morning!

Mary and I were completely crushed by God's kindness. Now, whenever we're tempted to grumble at God we remember that night when He rebuked us with kindness. This is a God who is worthy of respect!

Worthy Is the Lamb Who Was Slain

Jesus in His manhood is also worthy of our respect. Think of Christ's courage in laying down His life for us!

Men had given up their lives for others before Jesus was born, and men have given up their lives since, but Jesus stands head and shoulders above them all. For example, consider the men on the Titanic. When the Titanic hit the iceberg and started to go down, everyone began boarding lifeboats. The Titanic, because its designer thought it was unsinkable, was not equipped with enough lifeboats to evacuate as many passengers as it could hold. It was full to capacity on this, its maiden voyage. Who would get berths in the lifeboats?

With extremely few exceptions, all the men stood back and let the women and children board the lifeboats. These men were heroes, calmly facing near certain death in the freezing cold waters of the Atlantic Ocean. But they had the respect of the women and children. They had each other's respect. The men supported each other in their sacrifice. The Christians among them were at peace with their God.

Jesus faced the cross utterly alone. His disciples had run away. One had betrayed Him. Another had denied three times that he ever knew Jesus. The few women and men of His followers who watched Him die didn't know what was happening. They mourned for Him and pitied Him, but only He knew that He was dying for them. The leaders who looked on mocked Him and gloated over Him.

The most crushing weight of loneliness came when God Himself forsook Jesus. While He bore the sins of His people on that cross, God would have nothing to do with Him. God's favor had turned to wrath.

Jesus knew what the cross was going to be like. As He told the Jewish leaders, He could have called on legions of angels to rescue Him. When the pain got too great, He could have laid down His life prematurely. But He didn't. Jesus went through with it, all the way to the end, because *our* lives were at stake. This is sacrifice! This is courage!

Jesus deserves our respect and He deserves our obedience. Let's say you were crossing the street and didn't see a car bearing down on you and a complete stranger leaped from the sidewalk and pushed you out of the way, and got hit by the car himself. If he survived and asked you for a favor, wouldn't you grant it? Jesus deserves much more than just a favor. If you have been born again, He saved much more than just your life in this body—He saved you forever!

What did the New Testament Christians have that we didn't have? Simple—they had the faith of a little child. They saw God as God. In their eyes Jesus was not some kind of sappy pal who lives to bail us out of our problems. Christ to them was "high and lifted up," the King of the earth, as He appeared to the prophet Isaiah. They feared to offend Him and longed to serve Him. This went a long way to keep them from flirting with the devil. But they had one more thing besides—an almost incredible joy in the Lord. Turn the page to see how we can recapture that joy today.

🍎 13 🍎

Could Be Worse

*The world is so full of a number of things
I'm sure we all should be as happy as kings.*
                                   Robert Louis Stevenson

The joy of the Lord is your strength.
                                   Nehemiah 8:10

One of the cleverest children's books we ever got out of the library was titled *Could be Worse*. *Could be Worse* was about an old grandfather whose two grandchildren complained that whatever disaster happened, all he ever said was "Could be worse." The little girl cut her finger and Grandpa said, "Could be worse." The little boy lost his kite in a tree and Grandpa said, "Could be worse."

One day Grandpa overheard the young ones complaining about how boring Grandpa was—how he never did anything exciting or had anything exciting happen to him. So he called them over and told them all about what had happened to him the previous night: how a great big bird had snatched him out of bed and carried him to the other side of the earth. He then related how he had managed to find his way back before morning, totally exhausted. What did the kids say? "Could be worse!"

A lot of wisdom is bound up in that one phrase, "Could be worse." Those kids thought Grandpa was weird because that was his answer to every ill. But it's amazing how much comfort there is in meditating on how things might be worse than they are.

In Chapter One I showed how Satan shattered the peace of Eden by creating in Adam and Eve a false need for the tree of knowledge of good and evil. In the same way, Satan spoils our joy by getting us to concentrate on false needs—how things supposedly could be better for us. In this he is assisted by today's church which more often operates by the rule, "The squeaky wheel gets the grease," than the motto "To him who has will more be given." The church is spending so much time encouraging its problem people to keep on perpetually "struggling" with their sins and false needs that it doesn't have time to do its work.

"Could Be Worse" Thinking

One movement that has been touted as the solution to lack of joy in the church is positive thinking. Positive thinkers, possibility thinkers, and the like are always trying to get us to think on the positive side of things. "You mustn't think negative thoughts," they warn. "Negative thoughts are destructive to your self-image. If you want things to get better, you have to imagine them getting better. Picture in your mind what your life would be like if things were better. If you do a good job of imagining the possibilities, have enough faith in your vision, and act as if it will happen, 'god' will make it happen."

But what if it doesn't happen? Then we get discontented. Concentrating on how things could be better always makes us unhappy, because no matter how good things get in this fallen world, they could always get better. You buy your dream house which you have been waiting for for years. You had it built especially for you. You picked out the model. You picked out the colors. You move in and everything's beautiful . . . for a week. Then you start seeing how the place can be improved. It's the same way with the world. Once you start thinking, "Could be better," you'll never run out of things to complain about.

This is the problem with the modern theory of positive thinking. Teachers of positive thinking encourage us to concentrate our thoughts on our own wants. They say that all things are accessible if you think positively about them or visualize yourself having them, and that if you have enough faith there's nothing you want you cannot have. Positive thinking encourages us to indulge ourselves in the pursuit of false needs. It actually *causes* discontent!

Modern positive thinking is the opposite of Biblical thinking. Modern positive thinking leads us to say, "I can have all things if only I believe strongly enough." Its teachers encourage us to always concentrate on what we lack and be striving in our spirit to get it. If we can't get what we want, that becomes a problem and a sign of failing spirituality and we go to a psychologist to figure out what went wrong.

You want to be joyful? Forget positive thinking. Start by learning how to be content. Follow the example of Grandpa in that children's book and think about how things could be worse! Ninety-nine percent of the time things really could be worse. Only people like Job have to work their imaginations hard to figure out how things could be worse. "So a horse just stepped on your toe. Could be worse. It could have been a hippopotamus." "So you had a car accident. Could be worse! You're still alive!"

When you say, "Could be worse," you are humbly recognizing that God is in control of the world. What you really are saying is, "Could be worse, but it isn't." This makes you grateful to the God who has made things as good as they are and leads to rejoicing. When you say, "Could be better," you're complaining against God, and complaining leads to bitterness and rebellion.

Contentment and Guts

Isn't it odd? If you look on the "dark" side—how things could be worse—it makes you cheerful. If you look on the "bright" side—how things could be better—it makes you frustrated.

The exception to this rule is when some injustice or mess ought to be righted and you are legitimately doing something about it.

Admitting it "should be better"—meaning *you* are taking responsibility to do something about it—instead of it "could be better" takes guts. Admitting it "could be worse" when it isn't your job to change the situation calls for a contented spirit. So in any given circumstance we have two choices: contentment or guts.

David, writing as one of God's sheep in Psalm 23, is a wonderful picture of contentment. He is so joyful in the Lord he brags about it! "The Lord is *my* shepherd." He's a satisfied sheep. He doesn't go wandering for better food. He is content with the food and water his shepherd provides. Life isn't all a bed of roses either. There are enemies around. But David is not afraid because he knows his shepherd is nearby with his shepherd's rod ready.

Psalm 37 says the same thing: "Trust in the Lord and do good; dwell in the land and enjoy safe pasture." We don't have to fret because of wicked men. God will take care of them for us. He will make sure from His heavenly judge's bench that justice is done on earth. David tells us, "Delight yourself in the Lord and he will give you the desires of your heart." Be still. Don't fret. Don't get angry. The Lord is on the throne. God says, "Just trust Me, and be content." The meek, not the worrywart, will inherit the earth.

We do have to be careful, though, that contentment doesn't turn into complacency—that we don't become like some folks who are so laid back they've gone to sleep.

Sometimes God shows us a problem, not as a test of our trust in Him, but because He wants us to do something about it. If you are getting depressed and upset about a problem, continually complaining, "Why doesn't someone do something about this?" *you* very likely are the someone who should do something about it. God calls His people to work by a "burning" in their hearts (Jeremiah 20:9). So if you have heartburn over a real wrong that needs righting, perhaps it's your calling knocking at your door!

Depression, physical causes aside, is mainly caused by wanting what you shouldn't have or failing to do what you know you ought to do. That is why self-employed people like homeworkers so often fall prey to depression. It's so easy not to do what you are supposed to when you are your only boss! The only way out of this Slough of Despond is to face the mess you have let pile up to the sky, summon up your courage, and start digging into it.

Francis of Assisi's prayer sums up the whole matter: "Lord, give me the courage to change the things I can, the serenity to accept the things I cannot, and the wisdom to know the difference."

The Joy of the Lord Is Your Strength

"The joy of the Lord is your strength." Nehemiah first spoke these words to the exiles who had returned from Babylon to Israel. After they had built the wall and settled in their towns, everyone assembled at Jerusalem. Ezra and the other priests read from the law and explained the words to the people. Many of them wept as they listened to the words of the law. Nehemiah told them:

> Go and enjoy choice food and sweet drinks, and send some to those who have nothing prepared. This day is sacred to our Lord. Do not grieve, for the joy of the Lord is your strength. (Nehemiah 8:10)

The joy of the Lord is still our strength. It's the antidote to discontent. Satan is powerless against a contented Christian. If we, like David, are contented sheep who find our total joy in the Lord, then we will be able to "be strong in the Lord and in his mighty power."

It's easy to say, "Be joyful. God says you ought to have the joy of the Lord." But where does the joy of the Lord come from? How can you get it? To stop at the oughts does people no good. "Yes, I ought to be joyful, but I'm not. How can I become joyful?"

Remember the [Fill in This Blank] to Keep It Holy

How can you learn to be joyful in the Lord? Isn't there more to it than recognizing that things always could be worse?

This answer is going to surprise you. I can almost guarantee it! I'm not going to talk about mystical prayer exercises or giving every penny you own to world missions. Those may come later, but that is not how Scripture tells you to start digging for the joy of the Lord.

Believe it or not, the number-one, grade-A, best training ground for learning to be joyful in the Lord is keeping the Sabbath. Now I know this sounds odd, but don't run away just yet. I don't belong to any strange group and I'm not being legalistic. I'm simply going to share from Scripture and experience *why* a revival of Sunday-as-God's-day will make you joyful.

Here's why I said that keeping the Sabbath will increase your joy in the Lord. Isaiah 58 says,

> "If you keep your feet from breaking the Sabbath
>   and from doing as you please on my holy day,
> if you call the Sabbath a delight
>   and the LORD's holy day honorable,
> and if you honor it by not going your own way
>   and not doing as you please or speaking idle words,
> then you will find your joy in the LORD,
>   and I will cause you to ride on the heights of the land
>   [or "the earth"—the Hebrew can mean either land or earth]
> and to feast on the inheritance of your father Jacob."
>   The mouth of the LORD has spoken.

The Promise and the Blessing

Someone may say, "Hey, the Sabbath is just part of the ceremonial law that Jesus did away with in the New Testament." Christians have argued back and forth for centuries about whether we have to keep the Sabbath. I would like to point out that we have a *promise* in this passage, not a command. It is exactly the same kind of promise as the promise about tithing in Malachi 3:8. There God tells the Israelites they are under a curse because they are robbing him of His tithes and offerings. He then tells them to tithe and goes on to say,

> "Test me in this," says the LORD Almighty, "and see if I will not throw open the floodgates of heaven and pour out so much blessing that you will not have room enough for it."

The rest of the Malachi passage lists the Lord's promises to protect their crops if they tithe, and says that other nations will call the Israelites blessed and Israel a "delightful land."

Preachers today have no problem telling their congregations that God wants us to tithe and reminding them that God promises to bless tithers (another promise in Malachi), even though the New Testament epistles never command us to tithe at all. Most preachers quite rightly understand that a promise is a promise, and that God is not going to stop blessing that kind of faith today. New Testament Christians might go farther than the Old Testament saints, but we are never called upon to do *less*.

In exactly the same way, God's promise that we will

- find the joy of the Lord
- ride on the heights of the earth
- and feast on the inheritance of our father Jacob

if we keep His Sabbath is just as valid today as it ever was.

Let me explain why this is so, and how honoring Sunday as God's Day leads to great joy and delight in the Lord and power as we face the world.

Do You Really Love God? Here's How to Find Out . . .
First, the Sabbath is a test of whether you love God or not. During the time Mary and I were engaged, we went everywhere together. We talked for hours till all hours of the night. We were each other's best friend and madly in love. Despite all the prophecies in popular literature about how we would get tired of each other, we still stay up till all hours and talk. The

only difference is that now we have more in common than we did then, so we could actually talk for days if we didn't get tired. To spend a day with my Mary with no business to attend to would be a refreshing treat.

The Sabbath is an entire day to spend with God. We aren't supposed to encumber the day with any of the week's business, just tend to necessary meals. It's a day to get together with Christian friends, to worship the Lord, and to do good deeds. Sunday is a day for being with God and doing things for Him.

Spending a whole day with God should be a delight. God's command to suspend all other work and entertainments on that day is more permission than command . . . if you love God. If you find that spending a whole day a week with God is a burden, you can find out what your true gods are by seeing what you would rather do instead. If you have an opportunity to spend time with God and discover you don't want to, that you would rather do something else, you have broken the first commandment.

You might say, "But I always spend at least an hour at the beginning of each day in Bible study and prayer. I don't need a special day." This is all well and good, but an hour or even two hours isn't a fair test. You can spend the whole time looking forward to the treat of doing something else afterward. The important test during the week is what you do with your *free* time, not with your religious *duty* time. When you are in love with God, you'll find that your hour with God spreads into the next hour and that you stop only because you run out of time. When you become the kind of person who would rather pray, read the Bible, or talk about Jesus with someone than do anything else, then you'll move mountains.

If you find that your love is a bit thin, the necessity of learning to get along with God for a whole day without distractions is just the push your relationship with Him needs.

You Deserve a Break That Day

Second, the Sabbath is a day to get away from the devil and his messengers and get a true perspective on the world. Day-to-day work in the world constantly gives the devil opportunities for planting temptations to sin and worry. During the week you are almost constantly bombarded by the devil's propaganda, whether through television, or the newspaper, or the magazines you read, or the conversation of non-Christian colleagues, or billboards.

Sunday gives you an opportunity to clean all that out. You have no idea how much the world has infiltrated your thinking until you get a chance to step back from the constant propaganda barrage.

Let me share just one example from our own family's life. Over ten years ago we got rid of our television because we were shocked at the downslide in morals on even what used to be "clean" shows. The commercials also were beginning to flirt with blasphemy—"Let there be light" as the lead-in to a hair color ad, for instance. We also stopped reading the popular secular magazines for similar reasons, preferring to spend our free time with Christian classics and the Bible.

Several years later, I ran into a *Time* magazine in our seminary library with an article that featured bare-breasted models showing off some new clothing fashions. That really shocked me, as I hadn't been around to witness the previous steps of *Time's* slide into depravity. Nor was I prepared for the pro-homosexual articles, fawning reviews of pornographic literature, and all the other common fare of the new journalism. I wasn't ready for the nudity, sex, profanity, and blasphemy on television that had crept in during our media sabbatical, either.

It is good to be shocked by these things, because they are evil and shocking. I found, though, that most of my Christian friends didn't seem particularly upset by all this evil. That is why I got to write this book and they didn't!

Those of us who have indiscriminately continued to read and watch whatever the world provides lose our ability to be shocked. Evil starts to seem normal and harmless.

Consider the decency boycotts of TV shows. . . .

Christians:	We won't watch this trash for a month unless you clean it up a little.
The networks:	You mean you have been watching it until now?

Apparently so, according to the polls of professing Christians' TV-watching habits. We supposedly watch as much or more secular TV programming than the nonbelievers. Yet if twenty years ago anyone would have told you, "In the 1980s you will be watching TV shows that promote homosexuality, adultery, fornication, blasphemy, and drunkenness" you would have said, "No way!" It's because these things have crept in little by little that you haven't been able to notice the total sum of depravity you are now being asked to swallow.

I'm not asking you to trash your TV set and cancel your magazine subscriptions (although that might be a good idea!). All I'm asking is that you step outside the circle of the world's noise for one day a week. That's all. Just one day. One day without the TV, the radio, the sports, the newspaper, the magazines, the advertising, the shopping, the unnecessary driving, and all the other ways we find to plug our ears and blind our eyes to what God has to say to us.

"Be Still and Know That I Am God"—Psalm 46:10

You know, it's no accident that God tells us, "*Be still* and know that I am God." You can't hear God's "still, small voice" while you're listening to some hysterical announcer plugging a new brand of soap powder, much less while you're following the tangled sex lives of the implausible characters in some TV drama. The most common way church members spend Sunday afternoon—watching TV or reading the newspaper—is about the worst way to keep in touch with God that there is. Sunday as a Sabbath gives God a chance to get through, as well as a way for you to start breaking your addiction (now, let's be honest, for most of us it *is* an addiction) to the popular entertainment and information media.

The devil will not give you up easily. He will be right there every Sunday at first, reminding you of the big meeting on Monday, tempting you with the football game at four in which your team is playing, mentioning the pile of bills waiting to be paid, etc. The way to get rid of the devil is to start doing something with God. Start reading your Bible, or if you have kids, start reading it to them. Buy some hymnbooks and start singing some of your family's favorite hymns. Start talking with your wife about the things God has done for you in the past. Just start doing something with God. The devil, after testing you a few times to see if he can get you to stop, will leave.

Back before Mary and I met, when I was in college, I came home for a weekend to see my folks. The girl next door just happened to have also come home that weekend. We had hung around together a little in high school and I liked her, so I went next door to visit. The whole time I was there all she could talk about was some guy named Ward from school who I didn't even know. I soon got tired of hearing about Ward. Very soon, in fact. At the first polite opportunity, I excused myself and went back home. I haven't looked her up again since.

The devil feels the same way about God. If God is all you want to talk about, the devil will find more congenial company elsewhere.

Preventative Maintenance

Recently I was looking at copy machines, with an eye to finding one for our home business. One model I looked at had a light that turned on every 40,000 copies or so. When that light went on, the copier was saying that the time had come for preventative maintenance. Nothing was wrong with the copier. The copier could go on making copies, but the manufacturers of the copier had programmed that light to go on at selected intervals to tell the owner of the copier that now was the time to check the copier for problems before they occurred.

The Sabbath is not only a test of whether you love God or not and a chance to get away from the devil; it is also preventative maintenance time for our spiritual armor. During a battle armor gets dented or even broken. Every once in a while a knight has to visit the armorer and have his armor checked out and repaired. The Sabbath gives us a time between battles to check out and repair our armor.

The pieces of our armor are these, as outlined in Ephesians chapter 6:

- *The belt of truth.* We already saw how the Sabbath gives you a time to flush out the devil's propaganda and test it against God's truth.

- *The breastplate of righteousness.* The Sabbath gives you time to reflect on your behavior during the week and examine your righteousness for signs of slippage. It gives you time to let God check you out according to David's prayer in Psalm 139:23, 24:

  > Search me, O God, and know my heart;
  > test me and know my anxious thoughts.
  > See if there is any offensive way in me,
  > and lead me in the way everlasting.

- *Feet fitted out with the preparation of the gospel of peace.* If you have a good church to attend, you have the time and opportunity to hear the gospel preached. If not, you can get busy preaching it to others and trying to start a church!

- *The shield of faith.* You can renew your faith by proclaiming the Lord's death in the Lord's Supper. But failing that, just spending a day on God is an act of faith. Sane adults don't spend one day a week visiting with an imaginary friend.

- *The helmet of salvation.* A Christian who is behaving himself should never have trouble with his salvation. But you can lose a pair of glasses perched on top of your head. If you don't have time to remind yourself of your salvation you can begin to doubt it is there. Sunday is a day to reminisce on the family stories and specifically, to remember how you were saved.

- *The sword of the Spirit.* Sunday gives you the time you need to meditate on God's Word. I was a computer programmer before I became self-employed. I found I couldn't meditate on Scripture and write programs at the same time. But I didn't have to write programs on Sunday!

Practice, Practice, Practice

When a sergeant is teaching new recruits how to shoot, he doesn't do it by throwing them into combat. No, they practice shooting on a firing range with large, stationary targets. In the same way, a quarterback doesn't practice his passing by telling three 300-pounders to jump on him every time he throws the football. A golfer practices driving on a driving range and putting on a putting green. A tennis player practices his serve, alone, by taking a whole bunch of tennis balls to the court and serving them one after another. Then he gathers the balls together again and serves them again.

David could not use Saul's armor against Goliath because he wasn't used to it. He needed time to practice before he could use the armor in battle. Sunday gives us time to practice our sword play and shield work before we test them in the world. We get the chance to prove our armor in ideal conditions before we trust it in combat.

The Twenty-Four Hours of Power

Finally, those who keep Sunday as a Sabbath, not as a legalistic attempt to earn salvation but as a day to enjoy God, will be blessed with spiritual power. That is what the Bible says in Isaiah 58. Not only will you find the joy of the Lord, but God "will cause you to ride on the heights of the earth and to feast on the inheritance of your father Jacob."

What does it mean to ride on the heights of *ha-eretz* (the Hebrew for *land* and *earth*)? It means to have a position of power and authority. And what is the inheritance of our father Jacob? Physically it was the land of Israel, which stands as a Scriptural figure for the whole world. See for example how Jesus quoted Psalm 37:11, "The meek shall inherit the land." Jesus said, "Blessed are the meek, for they will inherit *the earth*."

That Jacob's inheritance is spiritual dominion over the earth is even clearer from Psalm 47:

> Clap your hands, all you nations; shout to God with cries of joy.
> How awesome is the LORD Most High,
> the great King over all the earth!
> He subdued nations under us,
> peoples under our feet.

> He chose our inheritance for us,
>   the pride of Jacob, whom he loved. . . .
> The nobles of the nations assemble as the people of the God
>   of Abraham,
> for the kings of the earth belong to God;
>   he is greatly exalted.

Jacob's seed now includes us as his spiritual seed, just as Christians are the spiritual seed of Jacob's grandfather Abraham (Romans 4, Galatians 3:29). And Jacob's seed will be the meek who inherit the earth.

Let's not get into a lot of arguments here. I'm not talking about Christians becoming the presidents of every country on earth or any such scheme. We're talking *spiritual* authority here—Christians triumphing over principalities and powers in the spiritual realm, with a corresponding effect in the physical realm.

As Christians have spiritual victory, we can expect to see a leavening effect in the world. Just all the bars in some sections of Wales closed when the Welsh Revival of 1904 hit, so we Americans and Canadians and Brits and Aussies can expect to see striking results in the lives of our communities when the church is revived.

A True Story

Mary and I have tasted this kind of spiritual victory. When we first became Christians, we were far from spiritually powerful. I was so apathetic I criticized nothing, and Mary was vocal in criticizing everything. (She was right most of the time, too.)

Although we both had degrees from prestigious institutions, in the church we seemed like third wheels. Nobody needed us for anything, not even for teaching a Sunday school class. At the same time, we couldn't find anyone who wanted to disciple us so someday we *could* teach a Sunday school class! As for our financial situation, we were living on $300 a month while we struggled to pay off past debts and attend seminary at the same time. This meant our clothing was just this side of ragged, which unhappily also meant (in the church we were attending at the time) that we found ourselves as more-or-less social outcasts. We also were carrying around a lot of baggage from our unsaved lives in the form of poor social graces, and that didn't help either!

Only after years of struggling without encouragement, studying the Bible and doing our best to conform ourselves to its teaching did we find the promise in Isaiah 58 about keeping the Sabbath. We got all excited about it and immediately started keeping Sunday for God. We got special Sunday toys for our two sons and started spending the day not only worshiping for an hour or two but also reading huge sections of the Bible, praying, singing Psalms, instructing our children in the things of God, and napping to recoup our physical strength.

Right at that time was when Mary felt God giving her the go-ahead to start writing what became *The Way Home,* her first book. She had been thinking about that project for years, but had never felt she had God's permission to start on it.

As a result of Mary writing *The Way Home*, she was asked to write one of the two responses to a paper to be presented at the Third Congress of the International Council on Biblical Inerrancy (ICBI). Later, the writer of the main paper became unable to finish it, so the ICBI committee asked Mary to write the main paper. Mary and I wrote the paper together and both our names appeared on it. I had the honor of presenting our paper at the conference.

Only seven years before we had been totally passed over by the church. Now we were being asked to present a paper before the evangelical church's most prominent scholars! Mary's first book also led to opportunities to write many more, including opening the door for this book of mine you are now reading. And it all began when we started to keep the Sabbath!

"Draw Near to God and He Will Draw Near to You"

This book is not meant to be a treatise on the Sabbath. The point is this: James tells us, "Resist the devil, and he will flee from you. Come near to God and he will come near to you." If you want to have the joy of the Lord and stop flirting with the devil, you have to come near to God.

Mary tells me that for several years she used to despair at this verse because she was going through a testing time, a "dark night of the soul." During that time she tried so hard to draw near to God but never felt like He had drawn near to her. But the Bible never said, "Draw near to God and He will leap to your side." There may be a lag between you drawing near and God drawing near—but He promises that He will if you will!

If Adam and Eve had truly delighted in being with God in the beginning, they would have had no problem with the devil. Their problem was trying to sneak off and do something on their own. They didn't want to ask God's permission. Like one of my little ones whom I caught doing something dubious one day, they were afraid to ask permission because they thought God would say no.

That is the problem with the modern Western church. We are trying to do something on our own, and we're afraid God would say no if we asked Him. We have to draw near to God and talk with Him more. We have to start somewhere! And the best time to start doing this is when you have the most time to spare—on Sunday.

Remember the story of Jim and Sue at the beginning of this book? What do you think will happen to Sue when she finally gets wise, starts spending her time with Jim, and kicks Nick out of her life?

You're right. Jim marries her and they live happily ever after.

Jim stands for Jesus, Nick stands for Satan, and Sue stands for us. Let's draw near to Jesus so He can draw near to us. If this means giving up some of our time, our comfort, and our way of doing things, let's do it!

Let's get busy taking care of our households and serving the Lord. We need revival more than we need pleasure, popularity, or power. We need the old gospel and the old cross more than we need a new church program or a new image. We need the joy of the Lord more than we need the fleshpots of Egypt. Flirting with the devil just isn't worth it.

Even so, come, Lord Jesus!